OFFICE FOR STANDARDS
IN EDUCATION

Handbook for Inspecting
PRIMARY AND
NURSERY SCHOOLS

with guidance on self-evaluation

ref:

This *Handbook* applies to the inspection of schools in England from January 2000

London: The Stationery Office

Published with the permission of OFSTED on behalf of the
Controller of Her Majesty's Stationery Office

Applications for reproduction should be made in writing to:
The Copyright Unit, Her Majesty's Stationery Office, St Clements House,
2–16 Colegate, Norwich NR3 1BQ

Second impression 2000

ISBN 0 11 350109 9

Inspection Quality Division
Office for Standards in Education
Alexandra House
33 Kingsway
London WC2B 6SE

Telephone: 020 7421 6800
Website: http://www.ofsted.gov.uk

CONTENTS

INTRODUCTION

This Handbook *is published by Her Majesty's Chief Inspector of Schools in England (HMCI) for use by inspectors of primary and nursery schools. Like earlier editions, the* Handbook *will also prove useful for school self-evaluation.*

The *Handbook* has been fully revised. It incorporates the requirements of the differentiated inspection system, in which the most effective schools are offered less intensive inspections than the rest. Both types of inspection lead to summary reports for parents, written to the same standard format, which form part of the longer reports.

The *Handbook* has three parts:

Part 1. Guidance on using the *Evaluation Schedule*
This presents the schedule for evaluating school effectiveness, which contains criteria or benchmarks against which schools can be gauged, together with guidance on collecting and weighing evidence to arrive at judgements.

Part 2. Guidance for inspectors on conducting inspections and writing reports

Part 3. Using the *Handbook* for school self-evaluation

INSPECTION

The *Handbook* shows how the inspection Framework, *Inspecting Schools*, should be applied in the inspection of nursery, primary and middle-deemed-primary schools. However, the central principles for recognising and judging the quality and standards of schools apply to schools of all types and sizes.

The guidance in this *Handbook* is intended to help ensure that the inspection process is of the highest quality and that judgements about a school are both fair and rigorous. A good inspection is one where:

■ judgements about the educational standards achieved at the school and the strengths and weaknesses in teaching and other aspects are secured by sufficient valid and reliable evidence;

■ the main findings, summarised at the front of the inspection report, together with issues which the school should address in order to improve, are clearly identified and reported to the school.

It is equally important that:

■ inspectors establish an effective working relationship with the school based on professionalism, sensitivity and an understanding of the school's concerns and circumstances;

■ the process of inspection is well planned and effectively managed;

- there are good communications with the school and individual staff, which lead to a clear and shared understanding of what is involved at each stage of the inspection;

- inspectors readily explore issues with staff through professional dialogue;

- feedback to the school, staff and the governing body, both orally and in writing, is clear and comprehensible.

Inspectors should leave the staff and governors feeling that they have gained from their contact with the members of the team, as well as recognising the thoroughness of the evidence base and understanding and respecting the judgements which emerge. Those involved in running the school should feel that the inspection has provided a valuable contribution to their strategy for improvement.

The new system of inspection applies from January 2000.

SHORT AND FULL INSPECTIONS

This *Handbook* describes a differentiated inspection system. The aim is to offer the most effective schools a SHORT INSPECTION. Other schools will have a FULL INSPECTION, which resembles the inspections carried out to the previous Framework. This differentiated inspection system reflects the Government's commitment to less intervention in schools which are more successful.

Similarities and differences

SHORT and FULL INSPECTIONS have many common features. Both must:

- report on the quality of the education provided by the school; the educational standards achieved by pupils in the school; the efficiency with which the financial resources available to the school are managed; and the spiritual, moral, social and cultural development of pupils at the school;

- result in an inspection report for the appropriate authority for the school, and a summary of the report for parents, written to a standard format;

- be conducted by inspection teams led by a registered inspector and including a lay inspector;

- use similar procedures before and after the inspection;

- continue to identify schools requiring special measures or having serious weaknesses, and to report when a school is underachieving.

The differences in the two types of inspection are that:

- only the FULL INSPECTION will lead to detailed reporting of each subject;

- the FULL INSPECTION needs to fulfil the requirements of the whole *Evaluation Schedule*, but the SHORT INSPECTION may omit some parts;

- feedback is offered to every member of staff during or at the end of FULL INSPECTIONS, but this is only done as far as is practicable, after lessons, in SHORT INSPECTIONS;

- teachers are provided with a profile of inspectors' judgements on their lessons after FULL, but not SHORT, INSPECTIONS;

- the SHORT INSPECTION will not necessarily cover the work of every teacher.

The purpose and nature of a SHORT INSPECTION

The SHORT INSPECTION provides an educational 'health check' of the school. The inspection samples the school's work rather than inspecting and reporting fully on each subject. In all but the smallest schools, fewer inspectors will spend fewer days in the school than in a FULL INSPECTION. A SHORT INSPECTION usually lasts for two or three days, whereas a typical FULL INSPECTION lasts for up to one week. The team normally consists of between two and five inspectors rather than involving as many as the seven or eight required in the FULL INSPECTION of large primary schools. Although a SHORT INSPECTION will normally endorse the quality and standards of an effective school, it may sometimes find that a school is underachieving, has serious weaknesses or even requires special measures. This will mean that it is likely to be subject to HMI monitoring and/or an early FULL re-inspection. The report from a SHORT INSPECTION will focus selectively on the school's strengths and areas where improvement is needed. SHORT INSPECTIONS should cause less pressure on the school because the number of lessons observed is considerably smaller than in a FULL INSPECTION.

The purpose and nature of a FULL INSPECTION

The FULL INSPECTION provides an evaluation of the entire school. This includes inspection and reporting on the main subjects of the curriculum by inspectors who have specialist knowledge of those subjects. The FULL INSPECTION leads to a report on every aspect of the school listed in the *Evaluation Schedule*.

Part 1 of the *Handbook* provides guidance on using and interpreting the *Schedule*. All inspectors must be familiar with this guidance. Registered inspectors must ensure that members of their teams who carry responsibility for the inspection of particular aspects of the school thoroughly understand and use the guidance that applies to these aspects. The guidance must be interpreted sensibly during an actual inspection; some parts will be more relevant than others to the inspection of a particular school. It is for the registered inspector to judge where the priorities lie and how best to use the time available.

Part 2 of the *Handbook* provides guidance on how to conduct inspections and write reports. The registered inspector must comply with this guidance and ensure that members of the team also observe it.

SCHOOL MONITORING AND SELF-EVALUATION

The criteria in the *Evaluation Schedule* provide a secure basis for school self-evaluation. OFSTED is committed to promoting self-evaluation as a key aspect of the work of schools. Monitoring and evaluation are essential if the school is to set priorities and decide the action to take to improve the school's quality and raise the achievements of its pupils.

OFSTED has already made three substantial contributions to self-evaluation by:

    i.   publishing *School Evaluation Matters*, which was issued to all schools;

    ii.   preparing annual *Performance and Assessment (PANDA) reports* for all schools;

    iii.   developing a pack for training school evaluators.

Part 3 of the *Handbook* provides schools with advice on how to make use of the *Evaluation Schedule* for their own evaluation.

PART 1

GUIDANCE ON USING THE *EVALUATION SCHEDULE*

Part 1 provides guidance for all inspectors and school evaluators on the use
of the Evaluation Schedule that is set out in the Framework, Inspecting Schools.
The Schedule helps you to find the answers to a set of eight questions about a school.

THE STRUCTURE OF THE EVALUATION SCHEDULE

The *Schedule* is arranged in a way that both reflects the evaluation sequence and defines the summary of the inspection report (*see Figure 1*). It highlights the distinction between the **standards** achieved by pupils at the school, or outcomes, and the factors which contribute to these outcomes, **provision**, particularly the quality of teaching, and **leadership and management**. In using each section of the *Schedule*, you should have regard for what is achieved by, and provided for, *all* pupils in the school, whatever their age, attainment, gender, background, ethnicity or special educational need.

Figure 1: Structure of the Evaluation Schedule

CONTEXT AND OVERVIEW

1. **What sort of school is it?**

OUTCOMES

2. **How high are standards?**

    2.1 The school's results and pupils' achievements

    2.2 Pupils' attitudes, values and personal development

QUALITY OF PROVISION

3. **How well are pupils taught?**

    4. How good are the curricular and other opportunities offered to pupils?

    5. How well does the school care for its pupils?

    6. How well does the school work in partnership with parents?

EFFICIENCY AND EFFECTIVENESS OF MANAGEMENT

7. **How well is the school led and managed?**

ISSUES FOR THE SCHOOL

8. **What should the school do to improve further?**

CONTEXT AND OVERVIEW

■ *What sort of school is it?* This section describes the school, summarises its quality and standards, outlines strengths and weaknesses and evaluates improvement since the last inspection.

OUTCOMES

■ *How high are standards?* This section contains two areas of enquiry.

- Evaluation of the school's results and achievements should focus on the school's results, trends in performance, and strengths and weaknesses in particular subjects. You should also judge how well the pupils achieve, that is, whether these pupils in this school are getting on as well as they should.

- The section on pupils' attitudes, values and personal development explores pupils' response to the school: their attitudes; behaviour; personal development and relationships, and attendance.

QUALITY OF PROVISION

This is covered in four sections, the first of which is particularly important.

■ *How well are pupils taught?* This question requires you to look at the quality of teaching and learning. At the heart of the criteria is the extent to which pupils are challenged and engaged in learning, and are learning at the right level.

■ *How good are the curricular and other opportunities offered to pupils?* This question is concerned with the quality and range of the curriculum, including provision for pupils' spiritual, moral, social and cultural development, and extra-curricular provision including study support.

■ *How well does the school care for its pupils?* This question focuses, in SHORT INSPECTIONS, on the active steps the school takes to ensure pupils' welfare, health and safety, and in FULL INSPECTIONS on the overall assessment, support and guidance arrangements.

■ *How well does the school work in partnership with parents?* This question examines parents' views of the school and the basis for these views and, in FULL INSPECTIONS, the range of parental involvement in, and links with, the school.

EFFICIENCY AND EFFECTIVENESS OF MANAGEMENT

Effective schools invariably have a clear sense of purpose, drive and direction, supported by efficient and effective management and administration.

■ *How well is the school led and managed?* This question covers a range of enquiries into leadership and management issues, in particular, approaches to enhancing the performance of staff and pupils; the role of governors and, in FULL INSPECTIONS, detailed questions about staffing, accommodation and resources.

THE STRUCTURE OF THE GUIDANCE ON USING THE EVALUATION SCHEDULE

Each section of the guidance includes five elements:

- The page from the *Evaluation Schedule*, as in the Framework, *Inspecting Schools*;

- *Inspection focus*, which amplifies the main evaluation and reporting requirements, stressing the features on which an evaluation must concentrate;

- *Making judgements*, which provides guidance on where to pitch your evaluations, drawing from, but not re-stating, the criteria;

- *Reporting requirements*, which spells out what is expected in the reports of SHORT and FULL INSPECTIONS. The summary of the report follows the same format in both;

- *Guidance on using the criteria*, which illustrates how you should interpret the criteria and test the evidence against them. The criteria amount to a set of standards representing good practice. They provide a basis for accurate and consistent evaluation and for the identification of strengths and weaknesses. In reaching overall judgements, all the relevant criteria should be considered.

You should use the *Guidance on using the criteria* as a source of reference. In using the guidance, you must focus on the central judgements required by the Framework and not pursue such a diverse range of issues that the inspection becomes unmanageable.

When reporting, you should avoid quoting criteria verbatim and should concentrate on the reporting requirements highlighted in the *Evaluation Schedule*. You must draw evidence into the report to illustrate or explain judgements, bring the report to life, and capture the individual characteristics of the school.

USING THE *EVALUATION SCHEDULE* ON SHORT AND FULL INSPECTIONS

The *Schedule* maps out the lines of enquiry for the evaluation of schools. In FULL INSPECTIONS, the school must be evaluated and reported on in terms of all elements of the *Schedule*. In SHORT INSPECTIONS, those elements enclosed in a box are not required. The reporting requirements are indicated by a hollow square (☐).

1. WHAT SORT OF SCHOOL IS IT?

Inspectors must report on:

☐ the characteristics of the school;

and evaluate and summarise:

☐ the effectiveness of the school, including the value for money it provides;

☐ the main strengths and weaknesses of the school;

☐ the extent to which the school has improved, or not, since the last inspection;

relating their findings to the specific nature of the school and its pupils.

INSPECTION FOCUS

The inspection report for both SHORT and FULL INSPECTIONS must capture, as succinctly as possible, at the beginning of the summary:

■ the main features or characteristics that describe the school;

■ your overall view of its effectiveness, particularly in terms of its standards and quality of provision, and the value for money it provides.

After these two opening paragraphs, the report must list:

■ the strengths and weaknesses of the school, set out as WHAT THE SCHOOL DOES WELL and WHERE THE SCHOOL SHOULD IMPROVE.

After analysing any changes in the school's performance since the last inspection, the report should state:

■ the extent to which the school has improved, or not, since its last inspection;

giving reasons for this judgement.

Only the first of these four elements, the characteristics of the school, is known before the inspection. The other three are summative judgements, decided corporately, normally at the final meeting of the inspection team.

MAKING JUDGEMENTS

☐ The characteristics of the school

The report must start by giving the size, type and nature of the school. It should describe the background and circumstances of the pupils who attend the school, including ethnicity, special educational needs and their attainment on entry. Additionally, you should mention other factors that may be relevant to the school's performance, for example, pupil mobility.

Example 1.1

Extract from a summary report on a nursery school with a diverse intake

The school has 26 four-year-olds who attend full-time, and 53 three-year-olds who attend part-time. There are three children who have special educational needs. The children come predominantly from Asian, African-Caribbean and European families. English is the first language for less than half the children. The other children speak Gujarati, Bengali, Cantonese, Arabic, Spanish or Japanese as their first language, but most understand some English.

The following table (*see Figure 2*) alerts you to the main points you need to consider when preparing your *Pre-Inspection Commentary* and planning the opening paragraph, INFORMATION ABOUT THE SCHOOL section, of the summary of the inspection report. The questions and prompts will be more relevant to some schools than others. You must use your judgement when deciding what to include in the full report. You should be guided by whether the information you include is relevant to the quality and standards of the school, and whether it is essential for current and prospective parents.

Figure 2: The characteristics of the school

Is it like other schools?	Refer as appropriate to: • number and age range of pupils; • gender of intake and any significant gender imbalance; • type; • any attached units, such as nursery or special educational needs; • extent of over- or under-subscription.
What is known of pupils' attainment on entry?	Note any: • variations in the attainment of pupils on entry, if known.
Does it have a specific designation?	Is the school designated, for example as: • a 'centre of excellence' or a 'beacon school'; • part of an Education Action Zone (EAZ), 'Excellence in Cities', an Early Excellence Centre or other group (*see Annex 4*)?
Where is the school located and to what extent does the intake reflect the school's location?	The school's context in relation to: • the background of its pupils; • whether the school serves its immediate area; • recent patterns of admission and transfer.
What is the proportion of pupils eligible for free schools meals?	Note: • how this compares with levels nationally and with similar types of schools (if known); • any trends with successive intakes.
What different groups are there in the school?	Note the numbers of: • pupils aged 5 and under and if they are in nursery, reception or mixed-age classes; • ethnic groups represented in the school in significant numbers, including refugee children and asylum seekers; • Traveller children; • pupils for whom English is an additional language (EAL) and number of EAL pupils who are at the early stages of learning English; • pupils with special educational needs (SEN), especially those with statements; • other identifiable groups, for example non-attending pupils.

☐ The effectiveness of the school

At the end of the inspection you need to summarise the team's view of how good the school is. You should substantiate this judgement, particularly in terms of the *standards* achieved by pupils by the time they leave, the quality of education, particularly *teaching*, and the *leadership and management* of the school. The **overall effectiveness** of the school is reported in the summary of the report, together with a comment on the *value for money* it provides (*see page 15*).

The effectiveness of the school is an overall judgement based on the standards pupils achieve, the quality of education it provides, its leadership and management, and how far it is improving. To reach a judgement about overall effectiveness, you will need to weigh up carefully the team's conclusions about the following indicators of effectiveness:

- how well pupils achieve, and their attitudes, values and personal development;

- the quality of education provided, particularly teaching;

- how well the school is led and managed;

- how far the school has improved or maintained very high standards since the last inspection.

In coming to your conclusions, you will need to take account of the characteristics of the school and the background of its pupils. You may find it helpful to collect together the team's corporate judgements which you have recorded in the *Record of Corporate Judgements* and place them on a table such as that below. You need to give due weight to each area, giving particular attention to how well pupils achieve.

Figure 3: Aid to judging effectiveness

Judgement recording grade		1	2	3	4	5	6	7	
STANDARDS									
Pupils' achievements are:	Excellent	★	★	★	★	★	★	★	Very poor
Attitudes, values and personal development are:	Excellent	★	★	★	★	★	★	★	Very poor
PROVISION									
The quality of education, particularly teaching, is:	Excellent	★	★	★	★	★	★	★	Very poor
LEADERSHIP AND MANAGEMENT									
Leadership and management are:	Excellent	★	★	★	★	★	★	★	Very poor
IMPROVEMENT									
Improvement or maintenance of very high standards is:	Excellent	★	★	★	★	★	★	★	Very poor
CONTEXTUAL FACTORS									
The context of school in the local environment is:	Very unfavourable	★	★	★	★	★	★	★	Very favourable
EFFECTIVENESS									
The overall effectiveness of the school is:	Excellent	★	★	★	★	★	★	★	Very poor

The following characteristics illustrate where to pitch judgements about the overall effectiveness of the school.

Very good or excellent	The school achieves the highest standards possible in most of its work. High proportions of pupils are keen to learn. There are no significant problems of behaviour or absenteeism. The teaching is consistently good, with much that is very good; and virtually all pupils progress very well. The staff constantly look for ways to improve the quality of their teaching, are imaginative and make challenging demands of pupils. There are very good arrangements to support all pupils and care for them, and the school has a strong partnership with parents and carers. The school is well governed and self-critical. It knows what it does well, where its weaknesses are and how to improve them. It has made significant improvement since its last inspection or has sustained high standards. It provides good or very good value for money.
Satisfactory or better	The school achieves standards that are at least as good as they should be. Pupils have good attitudes. Almost all the teaching is at least satisfactory and much is good or better, and pupils are learning well. The school has developed a curriculum that meets the needs of individual pupils and provides opportunities which benefit all pupils. There are sound care arrangements. The school keeps parents and carers informed about their child's progress and enlists their support. The school has made satisfactory improvement since its last inspection and responds adequately to the challenges or issues it faces. It is inclusive in its policies, outlook and practices, and is led and managed in a cost-effective way, providing at least satisfactory value for money.

However, if the judgement is that the school is **not as effective as it should be, poor or very poor,** then you must consider as a team:

- whether or not the **school is failing, or likely to fail, to give its pupils an acceptable standard of education, and thus requires special measures;**

- whether or not **the school, although providing an acceptable standard of education, nevertheless has serious weaknesses in one or more areas of its work;**

- whether **the school, although not identified as having serious weakness, is judged to be under-achieving.**

Any of these findings must *always* be *stated explicitly in the report* using the form of words highlighted above (*see Annex 2*).

Example 1.2

Extract from a summary report on a large primary school

St Paul's Primary School is a lively and friendly community where pupils achieve very high standards in reading, writing and mathematics. The quality of teaching is excellent. The headteacher, governors, staff and parents work closely together to achieve their simply stated aim: 'high standards for all'. The school has above-average income but provides very good value for money.

[Overall: an excellent school (1)]

Judging value for money

The value for money provided by the school is a composite assessment of its effectiveness and efficiency in relation to its costs. You can only make this judgement when you have considered all the other elements of the inspection.

Your judgements should be based on a careful weighing up of the team's conclusions about:

■ the overall effectiveness of the school;

taking into account the characteristics of the school and the background of its pupils. You should then relate these evaluations to:

■ the unit costs of the school and its cost-effectiveness;

taking account of the efficiency with which the school is run.

In broad terms, you should consider value for money as effectiveness set against costs, and this can be illustrated in a two-way table.

Figure 4: Value for money as effectiveness set against cost

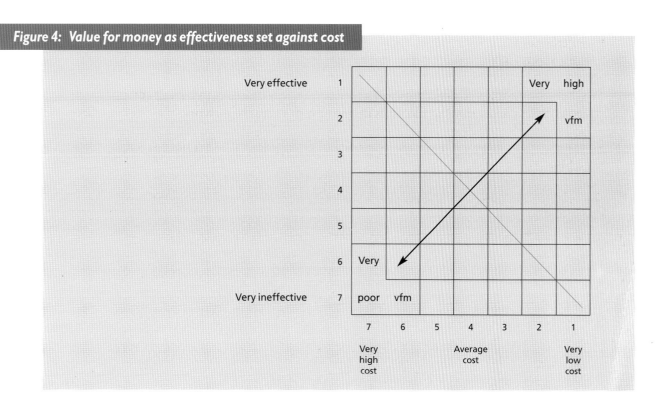

Put another way, you should consider the main judgement recording statement for the overall effectiveness of the school alongside contextual factors and the school's expenditure per pupil.

Judgement recording grade		1	2	3	4	5	6	7	
EFFECTIVENESS The overall effectiveness of the school:	Excellent	★	★	★	★	★	★	★	Very poor
CONTEXTUAL FACTORS The school and its pupils in the local environment:	Very unfavourable	★	★	★	★	★	★	★	Very favourable
UNIT COSTS The school's expenditure per pupil:	Very low	★	★	★	★	★	★	★	Very high
VALUE FOR MONEY The value for money provided by the school:	Excellent	★	★	★	★	★	★	★	Very poor

In **nursery schools,** overall effectiveness should be judged primarily in terms of the achievements of pupils and the quality of teaching, with reference also to the arrangements for pupils' care and the quality of links with parents. **Where the school does not manage a full delegated budget and unit costs are not known, no value for money judgement is required.**

☐ The main strengths and weaknesses of the school

At its final meeting, the team must corporately decide which aspects of the school are particularly good and which aspects are weak, if any. These should be recorded in the sections of the inspection report headed:

WHAT THE SCHOOL DOES WELL

and

WHAT COULD BE IMPROVED

The balance between these strengths and areas for improvement should reflect the overall quality of the school. The areas for improvement should form the basis for the issues for action to improve standards and quality, set out in section 8 of the *Evaluation Schedule*, WHAT SHOULD THE SCHOOL DO TO IMPROVE FURTHER?

☐ The extent to which the school has improved, or not, since the last inspection

Your evaluation of the school's current performance and your analysis of how the school has changed since its last inspection are integral to your judgement about its improvement. By the end of the inspection you must be able to report on how much improvement has been made and judge whether it has been enough. This overall judgement must relate to:

- how much change could reasonably be expected;
- what the school has done and if it has been enough.

You must give reasons for the overall judgement, drawing on illustrative evidence from different sections of the report. This should normally include, for example:

- trends in standards in the core subjects and whether the school is on course to meet or exceed its targets for English and mathematics;
- improvements in the quality of teaching and pupils' learning;
- how well the school's leadership has responded to the previous inspection, and what it has done to improve or maintain high standards and increase the cost-effectiveness of its provision.

How much change could reasonably be expected?

The previous report indicated what improvements were needed. The school may also have identified its own areas for improvement. How well has the school responded to these? You will need to consider the improvement made in terms of national trends in performance and the school's own targets, and any changes in the characteristics of the pupils who attend the school. Some schools will have done well to maintain very high standards or sustain the exceptional quality of what they provide. For all schools there is an expectation of either continued improvement or sustained excellence.

For FULL INSPECTIONS, each section of the commentary and each subject section should refer to the extent of improvement in the areas or subjects concerned, as applicable. In particular, you must consider standards, teaching, and leadership and management, as well as the school's ethos, in making your judgement.

The threshold for **expected** (that is 'satisfactory') **improvement** is illustrated by the presence of many of the following features:

In terms of the **standards achieved**, there is evidence of:

■ substantial improvement in attendance, attitudes and behaviour of pupils if these had been poor or unsatisfactory;

■ improved results in relation to national averages such that:
  - schools with low standards have improved more than the national average;
  - schools with average standards have kept pace with national trends;
  - high-performing schools have sustained high standards;
  - there are noticeable improvements, especially in English, mathematics and science;

■ improvement in relation to similar schools, such that:
  - schools which have had low performance approach the average;
  - schools which did relatively well sustain that position.

Schools whose performance, despite some improvement, still remains below the great majority of similar schools are unlikely to merit the 'satisfactory' judgement.

In terms of the **quality of education provided**, there is evidence of:

■ improved teaching in the areas where it was weakest;

■ a successful effort to consider and redress other areas of weakness identified in the previous report;

■ effective action on the main key issues, particularly those related to standards;

■ evidence that the school has monitored its progress.

In **leadership and management**, there is evidence of:

■ reported weaknesses having been overcome;

■ resources and expertise being directed towards priorities related to raising standards;

■ development of self-evaluation.

In relation to the **ethos** of the school, there is evidence that weaknesses have been overcome and there is:

■ general staff commitment to the achievement of high standards;

■ pupil and parent satisfaction;

■ good working relationships across the school.

What the school has done and has it been enough?

In making this judgement you will need to give greatest weight to any changes in the standards achieved by pupils, the quality of teaching, leadership and how the school is managed. The weighting you give to other changes will depend on the impact they have on the standards achieved.

Illustrate your judgement to show how change has been brought about. Reasons for change might include:

■ effective action planning;

■ the appointment of a new headteacher or other key staff;

■ the school's ability to identify and deal effectively with its own weaknesses.

A governing body is not obliged to address a key issue, but where it has not, it should have a convincing reason.

If you decide that the improvement has not been good enough, you will need to consider whether the school has serious weaknesses in one or more areas, or requires special measures to help it to improve.

Example 1.2

Extract from a summary report on an inner-city junior school

Since its last inspection in May 1996 the results achieved by 11-year-old pupils in the national tests have risen year on year. There has been a marked improvement in the results from Bangladeshi boys and the minority group of white boys. Most of the action points from the last inspection have been tackled well but teaching in information technology is still unsatisfactory.

[Overall: good improvement (3)]

Example 1.4 illustrates how the first five sections of the summary report might appear when completed in the way described in this section.

Example 1.4 Summary of the inspection report

ST PETER'S CE PRIMARY SCHOOL

[location including main post town]
Headteacher: [name]
Date of inspection: [start and end date]

Four inspectors, led by [name of registered inspector] inspected the school. This is a summary of the full inspection report, which is available from the school.

INFORMATION ABOUT THE SCHOOL

This school is a large voluntary controlled Church of England primary school for boys and girls 3–11 years old. It has 429 full-time pupils and 57 part-time pupils in its nursery unit. Taken together, pupils' attainment on entry is typical of that found nationally. Fifty-eight pupils have special educational needs; a figure lower than the national average. Nearly one-third of its pupils come from minority ethnic backgrounds (mainly African-Caribbean) and 21 pupils have English as an additional language.

HOW GOOD THE SCHOOL IS

St Peter's is a very effective school and makes extremely good provision for its ethnically diverse community. Pupils achieve very high standards because teaching is good and the work they do is demanding. The headteacher, governors and staff work together well to improve the school and maintain high standards. It provides good value for money.

WHAT THE SCHOOL DOES WELL

- Results in National Curriculum tests are very high, largely as a result of the school's commitment to all pupils achieving high standards
- There is a very strong community spirit that includes pupils of all ethnic backgrounds
- Pupils are very keen to learn; this makes a big contribution to the good progress they make in lessons
- Literacy and numeracy are well emphasised within a broad curriculum that extends out of school hours
- Pupils behave well and get on well with each other; all adults provide very positive role models
- Teaching is good and all staff constantly strive to improve
- The headteacher is a very effective leader and is well supported by governors and senior staff in managing the school and planning for the future

WHAT COULD BE IMPROVED

- The school's policy for checking the impact of teaching is not fully implemented
- The governing body does not have any way of checking that it provides good value for money when it makes decisions about spending
- Parents do not get enough information about the work their children do, their children's progress or the homework that is set

The areas for improvement will form the basis of the governors' action plan.

HOW THE SCHOOL HAS IMPROVED SINCE ITS LAST INSPECTION

When it was inspected last in February 1996 St Peter's was found to be a good and improving school. Since then it has continued to improve in many areas. The results achieved by its pupils in national tests at the age of 11 have risen year on year. Teaching has also improved. The school's increased emphasis on literacy and numeracy skills has brought about marked improvements in reading and mental arithmetic. All the action points from the last inspection have been tackled well, and improvements in teaching and in pupils' understanding of information and communications technology have been excellent.

2. HOW HIGH ARE STANDARDS?

2.1 THE SCHOOL'S RESULTS AND PUPILS' ACHIEVEMENTS

Inspectors must *interpret* and report on:

☐ the school's results and other performance data at the end of each stage of education, particularly in English, mathematics and science, highlighting any variations of achievement by different groups of pupils and in different subjects;

☐ trends in results over time;

☐ the school's progress towards its targets, including comment on whether the targets are sufficiently challenging.

Inspectors must *evaluate* and report on:

☐ standards of work seen, emphasising literacy and numeracy, and highlighting strengths and weaknesses in what pupils know, understand and can do;

- all the subjects inspected, focusing on the work of the oldest pupils at each stage;
- the variations between different groups of pupils and between subjects;

☐ **how well pupils achieve,** taking account of the progress they have made, the level of demand placed on them and other relevant factors.

In determining their judgements, inspectors should consider, where relevant, the extent to which:

- the results in National Curriculum and other tests match or exceed the average for all schools;

- children under 5 years are likely to attain or do better than the expected goals or standards by the time they start Year 1;

- the school is either maintaining very high standards or improving as expected;

- the school sets challenging targets and is on course to meet or exceed them;

- pupils with special educational needs, having English as an additional language or who are gifted and talented, are making good progress;

- standards are consistently high across subjects;

- there are no significant differences in the standards achieved by pupils of different gender or ethnic background;

- results in the school are high compared with those of similar schools (or show significant added value in relation to pupils' earlier results);

- pupils' attainment meets or exceeds the levels set by the National Curriculum and, where applicable, the local agreed syllabus for religious education.

INSPECTION FOCUS

The inspection report must give a clear and unequivocal interpretation of the school's results and how well pupils are achieving, giving reasons for these findings. Parents and others who read the report need an informed guide to the school's results: what they say about the school, how they should be interpreted, and how inspectors regard the achievements of pupils.

In this guidance we use the term *standards* to denote the educational attainment of pupils in relation to some clear benchmark, such as National Curriculum levels, or descriptions, at the end of a Key Stage. 'High standards', for example, means that a higher proportion of pupils of a particular age are succeeding at or beyond the level set than in the majority of schools. We also use standards in connection with other less measurable but broadly understood characteristics such as attitudes and behaviour.

Achievement, on the other hand, reflects the accomplishments of pupils in relation to what you would expect of those particular pupils. There are few clear reference points. Reference to terms such as 'ability' or 'aptitude' requires caution, for it is questionable what evidence you will have of such attributes. Prior attainment is a more secure reference point, if it has been measured, but essentially you should judge achievement by applying insight and expertise to all the evidence you have about the pupils, taking account of what they know, understand and can do, and what they are being asked to do. Broader indicators, such as measures that compare standards with those in similar schools and value-added measures, are also helpful in indicating the relative progress of pupils and providing a clue to how well they are achieving.

To judge standards you will have two main strategies. The *first* is to analyse the school's performance data before the inspection begins, unless it is a nursery school, in order to determine the pattern of results in English and mathematics by age 7 and English, mathematics and science by age 11. The data will also help you to judge whether the results are good enough when compared to all schools and those in similar circumstances, and indicate trends in performance over several years. This analysis should give an indication of some of the school's strengths and weaknesses and provide you with a starting point for the inspection.

The *second*, equally important, strategy, once you are in the school, is to find out for yourself what pupils know, understand and can do and assess how well they are achieving. Firsthand inspection evidence gives you the current picture of what pupils, including different groups of pupils, are doing well or not so well, and how effectively they are learning. **Your findings should be linked, through other parts of the report, with your diagnosis of what the school is doing to maximise pupils' achievements, particularly in terms of the quality of teaching. If there are differences between the performance data and what you see during the inspection, you should state these clearly and advance the likely reason(s).**

MAKING JUDGEMENTS

Before any inspection, you should analyse performance data printed in the *PICSI report* and any obtained from the school. The data will give you a picture of:

■ the school's results in tests and teacher assessments;

■ how the school's results relate to national averages and how they compare with similar schools;

■ how the results have changed in recent years;

■ other features of the school and the pupils it serves.

This analysis is not possible, of course, in the case of nursery schools.

The *PICSI report* for a primary school indicates, for example, whether results range from well above average, or very high, to very low, compared with all schools. The *PICSI report* also offers comparisons with similar schools. Gradings attached to these findings replicate *PICSI* grades A* (or 1) to E* (or 7). In all cases, you must interpret the school's results and explain whether they are satisfactory or not.

You may encounter schools with high, or very high, standards, which are nevertheless not high enough in some or all subjects, or for all groups of pupils. Here, reporting in terms such as 'the school achieves very good results in English and science, but attainment in mathematics, while above average, is not as high as it should be/not sufficiently high/too low' begins to make the link. You may find a school in which all results are 'well above average' but lack of success at the highest levels and/or the indifferent progress made from a high-achieving early stage may lead you to conclude that the results, while being well above average, are too low for the pupils concerned. In an underachieving school the *PICSI report* may reveal grades A or B for national comparisons and D or E for like school comparisons.

Performance data, however, do not tell the whole story about a school's standards. They relate to the past, not the present, and to year groups of pupils overall. The school may have undertaken monitoring by ethnicity, for example, or developed value added measures, which can inform your analysis. Your judgements therefore need to take account of all relevant evidence.

During the inspection, you can supplement and update your view of standards by:

- analysing the school's targets and the basis on which they have been set;

- identifying strengths and weaknesses in attainment in the subjects of the curriculum, judged by observations of lessons, discussion with pupils and analysis of the work they have completed and assessments made;

- reaching a view of how well pupils achieve on the basis of their earlier achievements, the work they are doing and the demands made on them.

Your evaluation of standards must pay particular attention to **competence in literacy and numeracy**, drawing on evidence across the curriculum, not just in literacy and numeracy sessions. You will need to consider whether pupils' skills in these areas are well enough developed to ensure they have full access to the curriculum or whether their skills are too low and are a barrier to learning. In FULL INSPECTIONS, you are required to report your judgements on all the subjects you inspect. Those subjects outside the core may be reported separately or together. Attainment in subjects must be referenced to the expected levels for the oldest pupils at each stage, in the years when they become 5, 7 and 11 (*see Example 2.1.1*).

Extract from the summary of an inspection report on a primary school

Throughout the school pupils achieve high standards in nearly all subjects, doing especially well by the time they leave. Standards in reading, writing and mathematics achieved by pupils aged 7 are higher than average and they match those of pupils in similar schools. Eleven-year-olds attain very high standards in English, mathematics and science, and do better than pupils in similar schools, especially in mathematics. The school's recent emphasis on literacy and numeracy has helped raise standards. In music, where teaching is outstanding, pupils sing exceptionally well. Standards in art are satisfactory up to the age of 7 years, but the work produced by 8–11-year-olds is limited to drawing and its quality is not high enough. This is because teachers have a poor understanding of the subject.

[Overall: very high standards (2), good achievement (3)]

Always explain if your judgements on the basis of firsthand inspection evidence differ in some way from your interpretation of the data about the core subjects (*see Example 2.1.2*). Detailed explanation is best given in the relevant subject section in the report of a FULL INSPECTION.

Extract from the subject section of a full inspection report on a primary school (explaining differing judgements)

There is some evidence of improvement in standards in mathematics in Year 2 despite the below-average national test results. The work in the pupils' books shows a marked difference in quality since the appointment of a new teacher. For example, her analysis of the test results identified several weaknesses, such as pupils being too slow to finish the paper and having difficulty with questions involving subtraction. The introduction of regular mental mathematics, practice sessions and tests has improved greatly their speed of work. The introduction of personal targets has motivated pupils, and their books show they have covered a greater quantity and wider range of work than the pupils in Year 3.

[Overall: satisfactory achievement (4)]

When judging pupils' achievements, use as your starting point the grade provided in the *PICSI report* that compares the school's performance with similar schools and any value added data. Your main evidence comprises your judgements of attainment and progress in lessons, pupils' work and the demands posed by the teaching.

The following characteristics illustrate where to pitch your judgements about results (first ☐) and *how well pupils achieve* (fifth ☐) in primary schools.

	Results	Achievements
Very high or excellent	Results are well above average or almost all pupils are on course to meet or exceed: learning goals by the end of Reception; National Curriculum Level 2 in English, mathematics or science by 7; and Level 4 by 11 years. Standards of literacy and numeracy are very high.	Most pupils are working at or near their capacity and achieving well in terms of their earlier attainment. Standards are higher than in similar schools and work in lessons is demanding. There is much added value.
Sound or better	Results are at least average, compared with all other schools and current work indicates standards are rising. Standards in literacy and numeracy are adequate for work in other subjects. Standards in other subjects of the National Curriculum are usually sound for pupils of the particular age.	Pupils are making satisfactory progress and achieving at least as well as in most similar schools. Almost all teaching is at least satisfactory but there is scope for greater challenge.

However standards (results and/or achievement) are **unlikely to be satisfactory** if any of the following features are present (*see Example 2.1.3*):

- the school's results are low in relation to similar schools;

- from the work seen there is evidence of low achievement in English and mathematics in the school;

- the trend of improvement in test results is lower than the national rate (unless the results are already high);

- there is evidence of widespread underachievement by particular groups of pupils, such as boys, girls, gifted and talented pupils, minority ethnic pupils or pupils with special educational needs;

- pupils' skills in literacy and numeracy are too low to cope with the current curriculum and do not adequately prepare them for the next stages of education.

Example 2.1.3

Extract from a full inspection report on a junior school

By the age of 11, standards in English are not high enough. In national tests, under half of the pupils reach the standards expected of 11-year-olds. Standards in English are lower than those attained by pupils in similar schools. This has been the picture for the last three years. Pupils' writing and spelling are particularly poor and this affects the quality of their work in other subjects. The school has done little to identify and remedy these weaknesses, particularly in teaching, which is still undemanding and pays too little attention to the sounds and structures of different words.

[Overall: low standards (6)]

In all cases make sure you give reasons for your judgements and link these judgements with what you are finding in other aspects of the inspection, so that you provide a consistent message throughout the report. For example, if teaching throughout the school is satisfactory or better, yet the school's standards are too low, you must interpret these apparently conflicting findings in clear and convincing terms (*see Example 2.1.4*).

Example 2.1.4

Extract from an inspection report on an infant school

Standards in mathematics and English are low and this is reflected in the below-average results in national tests over the last three years.

The pupils over the last three years have come into the reception class with very low skills in speaking and listening, and many have difficulty in relating to each other and adults. This affects their ability to get on with the tasks expected of them. The teaching is good throughout the school and enables pupils to improve, some of them very well, but is not able to compensate fully for the low starting point of many by the time the children leave the school. The school, nevertheless, compares well with similar schools.

REPORTING REQUIREMENTS

SUMMARY REPORT	On all inspections of primary schools you must complete the table headed STANDARDS provided in the summary to show results at the highest applicable Key Stage. For nursery schools, provide a summary judgement about pupils' attainment in relation to the early learning goals, particular strengths and weaknesses in the standard of work seen and how well pupils achieve.
	For primary schools give a brief interpretation of the results and evaluation of: the strengths and weaknesses of the school's performance, trends over time, progress towards targets, standards of work seen, and how well pupils achieve. If any of these are a feature of improvement in the school, record this in the section HOW THE SCHOOL HAS IMPROVED SINCE ITS LAST INSPECTION.
	Any achievements in subjects or areas of work that are particularly good or need to improve must be reported under WHAT THE SCHOOL DOES WELL or WHAT COULD BE IMPROVED.
SHORT INSPECTIONS	Expand in the commentary any items featured in WHAT THE SCHOOL DOES WELL or WHAT COULD BE IMPROVED. Complete the data tables at the back of the report.
FULL INSPECTIONS	Report fully under the section headed HOW HIGH ARE STANDARDS? THE SCHOOL'S RESULTS AND PUPILS' ACHIEVEMENTS. Complete the data tables at the back of the report.

GUIDANCE ON USING THE CRITERIA

☐ The school's results and other performance data

Do the school's results in National Curriculum and other tests match or exceed the average for all schools? Are children who are 5 years or under likely to attain, or do better than, the expected goals or standards by the time they start Year 1? To what extent do pupils' attainments meet or exceed the levels set by the National Curriculum and the local agreed syllabus for religious education?

For pupils of 5 years and under, your initial views on standards are likely to be based on information supplied by the headteacher, which may include baseline assessment data. For pupils of 5 years in the reception year, baseline data should be available from the school.

Using the information from the *PICSI report*, find out how well pupils have performed in the core subjects in **relation to all schools**. The letter grade, signifying this performance, must be reported in the summary report. Remember that this grade represents overall standards and that it may mask some important variations between subjects, aspects of subjects, or groups of pupils. Look also at data provided in the *PICSI report* which shows the proportion of pupils in the year group that achieved different levels in each subject. Note carefully how the school's distribution of results **compares with the proportions for all schools** for each stage and how the distribution of results compares **with similar schools**. This must also be reported in the summary report by a letter grade unless exceptional circumstances exist in which reporting the *PICSI* grade would give an unfair picture of the school.

In these circumstances, the team has discretion to change the comparative grade by one grade. Before making such a change, the team should consider carefully the evidence available to support a change of grade, taking particular note of any proper value-added information available. If it is considered that a change of more than one grade is needed, then OFSTED must be informed and the supporting evidence submitted.

You should examine the information in the *PICSI report* to find out:

- how well pupils attained in reading, writing and mathematics at 7 years;

- how well pupils attained within subjects, for example in reading compared with writing, at 7 years;

- how well pupils attained in English, mathematics and science at 11 years;

- how well pupils attained in one subject compared with another;

- how well boys' attainment compared with girls' in relation to national averages.

Discuss with the headteacher of a school serving more than one significant ethnic minority group any other significant variation in attainment by different groups of pupils.

Before the inspection, make sure you understand, in detail, the characteristics of the school. Take full account of the information in *Forms S1* and *S2* as they provide important details about the pupils. You need to do this in preparation for interpreting the data. You should be aware of the extent to which small numbers of pupils reduce the confidence you can have in results as an indicator of performance. Consider whether **high pupil mobility** affects the picture of the school's performance by asking for evidence of such pupils' attainment on entry to the school, and by judging what effect, if any, this has on the school's performance.

☐ **Trends in results over time**

Is the school either maintaining very high standards or improving as expected?

When inspecting nursery schools, gauge the standard of the work that you see during the inspection. You may not be able to determine trends but there should be some work that relates to targets for individual pupils. Nursery schools should be adding value and have some evidence to show you how they are doing this.

In primary schools you should examine any performance **trends** over time, and:

■ how well the school has improved **compared with all schools**;

■ whether the performance in any **subject** is persistently lower than in others;

■ whether the performance of **girls in relation to boys** is different from that found nationally;

■ any significant variation in performance by **particular groups of pupils.**

See if results of teacher assessments are broadly in line with the National Curriculum results. Discrepancies may indicate important factors such as low expectation or over-grading. Once you have assessed all the data, pose some questions (*see Example 2.1.5*) and begin to make hypotheses about the school's performance.

When you visit the school before the inspection, ask how the school analyses its results to identify strengths and weaknesses and whether it monitors the results of pupils from minority ethnic backgrounds and any other group; check what action it is taking in the light of this evidence. For example, what is done where a school has many pupils in the 'working towards' category when tested at the end of Key Stage 1? Find out about any pupils in the year group who were not assessed by teachers, or who did not take the National Curriculum tests. If there were many absences you need to take this into account in interpreting the data.

Example 2.1.5

*Extracts from the **Pre-Inspection Commentary** on a small primary school*

- *PICSI data indicate standards are consistently high at the end of KS1 over three years. Test results for KS2 are high but fluctuate from year to year, and mathematics results dropped significantly last year.*

- *The head's view that test results reflect the variation in ability in KS2 year groups over the last three years, whereas the KS1 results have been stable, suggests a superficial analysis of standards and does not explain why this affects KS2 but not KS1.*

Issues for further exploration:

- *What is there to substantiate the HT's view that changes in the ability of cohorts have affected KS2 results?*

- *The maths results were not as good as those in EN and SC last year. Does that reflect on the Q of T or is there another reason?*

☐ The school's progress towards its targets

Does the school set challenging targets and is it on course to meet or exceed them?

Evaluate how well the school collates and presents its results and other performance data so that they can be understood easily by those concerned, for example parents and governors. Find out if the school has analysed all its data to set targets in English, mathematics and science and taken action to make any necessary improvements (*see Example 2.1.6*).

The governing body, with the headteacher, will have agreed targets with the LEA to raise standards in English and mathematics. Many schools will also have set targets in other areas of the curriculum and for particular pupils and groups. To judge whether the targets are appropriate, you should evaluate the extent to which the school has:

- used its performance data to see how it compares with similar schools;

- formed an accurate appraisal of the extent to which any pupils are underachieving;

- identified the strengths, and particularly any weaknesses in teaching and learning in the core subjects and taken action to improve weaknesses;

- analysed its performance data in detail to see which aspects of subjects need most improvement;

- assessed the need for targets in non-academic areas such as behaviour;

- set aspirational targets which in your view should nevertheless be just achievable.

Example 2.1.6

Extract from the* Inspection Notebook *of the inspector responsible for English in an infant school

- *School's target to double the number of pupils at L3 and halve the number attaining L2c is ambitious [S/W? Check this out]*

- *EN co-ordinator has very clear and realistic plan to improve teaching [S]*

- *Parents know about the targets and have agreed to work with their children for 20 minutes a day to improve reading [S]*

- *Literacy strategy has improved teacher's knowledge [S]*

- *BUT too little attention given to improvements needed by individual pupils [W]*

- *Therefore school unlikely to achieve its target [W]*

Pay particular attention to the school's or LEA's analysis of data to find out differences in the **performance by different groups of pupils,** for example:

- boys compared with girls;

- pupils from minority ethnic backgrounds;

- gifted and talented pupils.

Look for evidence of whether the school has identified particular groups of pupils that are performing relatively less well than others (*see Example 2.1.7*).

Example 2.1.7

> **Extract from an Evidence Form *recording an interview with a middle school English co-ordinator***
>
> *School's analysis of writing shows that, in Key Stage 2, the African-Caribbean boys are attaining standards below those of their peers. Teachers talked to the pupils about their work and observed one another teaching to see if they had different expectations of these pupils. The staff, together with an external consultant, reached the view that the work given to these boys was not sufficiently challenging or interesting to motivate them to do well. The school's new approach to the teaching of writing includes lessons from writers in the local community, the headteacher and the English co-ordinator. Pupils across the whole of Key Stage 2 comment positively on the changes. Lesson observations and pupils' work show that the A–C boys in Year 6 now match the good standards of writing produced by their peers.*

☐ **Standards of work seen**

In SHORT INSPECTIONS, inspectors should judge attainment in lessons wherever they are confident of doing so competently, and always in the core subjects of English, mathematics and science.

In FULL INSPECTIONS only, you will need to undertake a more detailed evaluation of:

■ standards in all subjects inspected, focusing on the work of the oldest pupils in each stage;

■ variations between the standards of different groups of pupils and between different subjects.

Are standards consistently high across subjects?

During the inspection, evaluate standards by reference to **Early Learning Goals and the expected levels set by the National Curriculum.** Give priority to making judgements about pupils' skills in literacy and numeracy. In SHORT INSPECTIONS, make sure you have enough evidence to report on what pupils do well or not so well. Look for any examples of outstanding achievement, say in art, music or physical education. Also look out for clear gaps in pupils' knowledge, understanding or skills.

In FULL INSPECTIONS, make sure you have sufficient evidence to evaluate standards in English, mathematics, science, and information technology **in relation to the expected levels** and in religious education (where it is inspected) **in relation to the locally agreed syllabus.** Concentrate on the **oldest pupils at the end of each stage.**

In all inspections you should plan the best way of securing the evidence you need to evaluate standards. You need to do this in liaison with the school. The quantity of the evidence is much less on SHORT INSPECTIONS so you must identify what needs to be done at the pre-inspection stage to make sure you capture essential evidence.

Gather evidence by:

- observing and talking to pupils in lessons;

- listening to pupils asking and answering questions in plenary sessions;

- analysing the work they have produced;

- looking at records of attainment;

- questioning and talking to groups of pupils;

- talking to co-ordinators and looking at records together;

- looking at school portfolios of 'levelled' work.

When you evaluate standards of literacy and numeracy, find out how well pupils use their skills in other subjects, or whether their understanding of important aspects of these subjects is hindered by poor literacy and/or numeracy skills.

On *Evidence Forms*, make sure you record pupils' strengths and weaknesses within and between subjects so that you can accumulate a picture of the school's performance.

Bring all of your evidence together so that you can make an overall judgement. You will need to estimate the proportion of pupils who are on course to **achieve or exceed the expected goals by the end of the Reception year, or the expected levels or end of each Key Stage descriptors in the National Curriculum at 7 or 11**. Then you are in a position to judge how high standards are.

You should compare your judgements on standards in the core subjects with the results of end of Key Stage tests or other assessment data. If there are differences between your findings and the data, you should explain why this is so.

Are pupils with special educational needs, those with English as an additional language or who are gifted or talented, making good progress? Are there significant differences in the standards achieved by pupils of different gender or ethnic backgrounds?

Throughout both SHORT and FULL INSPECTIONS you should make sure you focus on **how well different groups of pupils are performing**. Start with any assessment data the school has to guide your observations. If the school cannot provide any analysis of data, make sure you check in lessons and from pupils' work how well different groups are doing. If your observation of pupils' work leads you to suspect that a particular group of pupils is achieving at a relatively higher or lower level, gather sufficient evidence of what pupils know, understand and can do to substantiate and exemplify your judgements. Since SHORT INSPECTIONS are designated for the most effective schools, such schools may have a clear view, supported by evidence of the performance of different groups. This should make your task easier. But check the school's view by focusing in particular on such pupils.

In FULL INSPECTIONS, particularly, your judgement about the achievements of pupils with SEN, pupils who speak English as an additional language, and gifted and talented pupils, should be summative judgements based on how well a sample of pupils are doing in relation to specific targets or goals.

You should ensure that the sample chosen is representative of the types of need found in the school and is also representative of the number supported, as defined by the *Code of Practice on SEN*, including pupils attending a diagnostic unit or resource base. When judging the **achievements of**

pupils with special educational needs, find out how the school uses its baseline assessment data, test and other assessment data, and target setting procedures in individual education plans (IEPs) or in statements, to set appropriately challenging targets for groups of special educational needs pupils. This will help you judge whether the **progress made is good enough.** Obtain different types of evidence, for example progress from records, pupils' responses to questions in class and their performance across the full range of subjects, as well as how well they are learning in small groups and in one-to-one teaching.

All this evidence should help you come to an overall view about the **achievements of pupils with special educational needs,** taking account of their progress towards the targets specifically set in IEPs or annual reviews. Make sure you record on *Evidence Forms* the gains pupils make in knowledge, skills and understanding, so that you can substantiate and illustrate your judgements, making a distinction here as appropriate between pupils with specific needs (*see Example 2.1.8*).

Example 2.1.8

Extract from the report of a full inspection of a primary school

Those pupils having moderate learning difficulties do not make the progress they should and achieve standards that are too low, particularly in reading and writing. Too little detail on their needs is included in their individual education plans and their targets are not clear. As a result many do not complete the work they are set and they lag further behind other pupils of their age.

[Overall: poor achievement (6)]

To judge the achievements of gifted and talented pupils, find out if the school uses its assessment data to identify their needs and make provision for them. In schools which appear to have few high attainers, check from your observations of pupils' work in lessons, and by talking to pupils, whether the results and the school's assessment data accurately reflect pupils' aptitudes.

In schools where **gifted and talented pupils** are identified, be sure you gather sufficient evidence to judge whether they are doing the sort of work of which they are capable, or working well below their capacity. In schools where such pupils are present but not adequately catered for, gather sufficient evidence to substantiate judgements about their underachievement (*see Example 2.1.9*).

Example 2.1.9

Extract, showing weaknesses, from the Record of Corporate Judgements in the full inspection of a junior school

Insufficient achievement by most able pupils:

- *in half of 48 lessons seen, low expectations resulted in underachievement [EFs]*

- *in all year groups, EN and MA activities do not challenge the pupils [EFs in EN and MA]*

- *in Y5, teachers praised copied work [Y5 EFs]*

- *parents concerned about low level of challenge for able pupils [parents' meeting, parents' questionnaire]*

- *little distinction in the work produced by average and high-attaining pupils*

To evaluate the **achievements of pupils who speak English as an additional language**, you should find out their competency in English by reference to the levels in the National Curriculum, as this will determine the kind of help they need. Gather sufficient evidence from lessons where these pupils are receiving support, or from any specialist teaching, so that you can make judgements on their progress and what they have achieved (*see Example 2.1.10*). Make sure you record on *Evidence Forms* gains in all aspects of English to substantiate your judgements. For further guidance see *Inspecting Subjects 3–11*.

Example 2.1.10

Extracts from an** Evidence Form **recording an observation in a nursery unit in which 20 pupils, 8 of whom speak Punjabi, work with a class teacher and a bilingual learning support teacher

Context:

Learning support teacher translates simultaneously. Objectives – to increase pupils' understanding and use of adjectives and to increase their awareness of the importance of listening.

Evidence:

Planning detailed and based on ELGs. Good relationships. Good range of Indian, African and European clothing. Simultaneous translation supports learning well. By the end of the lesson Punjabi pupils know and use correctly the English words 'dress', 'jacket', 'trousers' and 'shoes'. Most pupils listen carefully when others speak but three boys demand and receive a great deal of the language support teacher's attention. Her immediate response to their demands undermined the listening objective. EAL pupils make good progress in acquiring new vocabulary but very little progress in listening. Communicative language competence is too low.

[Overall: satisfactory (4)]

☐ **How well do pupils achieve?**

This is an important judgement for which you have a range of evidence.

In the classroom, you will find out:

■ what pupils know, what they understand and what they can do, and you should test their understanding and ability to apply their knowledge to related problems;

■ how pupils are responding to the educational demands made on them and whether they are challenged enough;

■ what work they have done, and to what standard.

Additional evidence should include:

■ how the school's results compare with similar schools;

■ tests, assessments and other records which show progress over time;

■ value-added measures if available.

You should also take into account other factors which help decide whether achievements are as high as they could or should be, for example:

- any special educational needs which have been identified;

- whether pupils' education has been disrupted by frequent changes of school;

- whether the fact that English is not the first language poses barriers to progress.

Achievements are likely to be high where pupils are working at full stretch, constantly engaged in thinking or doing things which are unfamiliar and which require effort, concentration and perseverance. Achievement is likely to be too low if pupils either fail to understand their work and what is expected (*see Example 2.1.11*), or they are consistently successful at tasks which they have already mastered. You should consider whether pupils have made as much progress as possible from the time they joined the school, as well as how well they apply themselves to their work.

Example 2.1.11

Extract from a report on a junior school

Pupils are not achieving enough in mathematics even though the school's national test results are above average at 11 years. Much of the work they are given in Years 5 and 6 is undemanding and does not make use of the skills they learnt in Years 3 and 4. They are not receiving enough stimulating work to extend their thinking, and more able pupils are held back.

[Overall: poor achievement (6)]

2.2 PUPILS' ATTITUDES, VALUES AND PERSONAL DEVELOPMENT

Inspectors must evaluate and report on pupils':

☐ attitudes to the school;

☐ behaviour, including the incidence of exclusions;

☐ personal development and relationships;

☐ attendance.

In determining their judgements, inspectors should consider the extent to which pupils:

- are keen and eager to come to school;

- show interest in school life, and are involved in the range of activities the school provides;

- behave well in lessons and around the school, and are courteous, trustworthy and show respect for property;

- form constructive relationships with one another, and with teachers and other adults;

- work in an atmosphere free from oppressive behaviour, such as bullying, sexism and racism;

- reflect on what they do and understand its impact on others;

- respect other people's differences, particularly their feelings, values and beliefs;

- show initiative and are willing to take responsibility;

- have high levels of attendance and low levels of unauthorised absence.

INSPECTION FOCUS

This section is concerned with how well pupils respond to school in terms of their attitudes to learning, their behaviour, their values and personal development. The criteria cover pupils' responses to what the staff provide, through their teaching and personal example, the curriculum, and the school's provision for spiritual, moral, social and cultural development.

The first experiences young children have of school are extremely important in developing positive attitudes to learning. You must judge how well they learn to behave and relate to others within a 'school' context. For all pupils, good behaviour is a pre-requisite for effective learning.

You also need to evaluate pupils' attitudes and their impact on how they learn and the standards they achieve. Attitudes are strongly influenced by what teachers do. You will learn much about the ethos of the school by observing the quality of relationships between pupils from different backgrounds and between pupils and staff.

MAKING JUDGEMENTS

Make full use of the parents' meeting and discussions with pupils to gain their perspectives on what it is like to be a pupil in this school. If pupils enjoy coming to school, find out what it is about the provision that makes this so.

Use your evaluation of pupils' attitudes in lessons and your contacts with, and observations of, them at other times to decide how good attitudes and behaviour are in this school. You will need to find out the extent to which attitudes and behaviour help or hinder pupils' learning. In making your judgement about the values and personal development of the pupils, take into account your conclusions about how well the school provides opportunities for pupils' spiritual, moral, social and cultural development, and how the school helps pupils develop into responsible individuals, and relate well to each other.

The following characteristics illustrate where to pitch judgements about the attitudes, values and personal development of pupils.

Very good or excellent	Pupils are eager to come to school and are quickly and positively involved in a wide range of activities. They behave very well in and around the school and work constructively and co-operatively in groups and productively on their own. They enjoy learning and are reluctant to stop when they have to. Pupils are tolerant of each other, and show a mature and growing understanding of each other and of different viewpoints. Behaviour and punctuality are excellent. The attendance figures for the school are at or above the national average, and there are no exclusions.
Satisfactory or better	Most pupils like school and the youngest are mainly confident in leaving their parents or carers. They are willing to help each other, teachers and other adults and take part in activities outside lessons. Most pupils behave well most of the time and they are able to work on their own. Pupils are kind and considerate and show an increasing respect for each other and a willingness to listen. They are punctual to lessons and rarely absent.

However, attitudes, values and personal development **cannot be satisfactory** if there are more than isolated instances of:

- disruptive, aggressive or intimidating behaviour;

- racist attitudes or sexist language or behaviour;

- marked unruliness in more than one class.

Example 2.2.1

Extracts from a report on a short inspection of a large primary school

The older pupils are confident and highly motivated learners. They have great pride in their achievements and they apply what they have learned to new work. Pupils listen to each other as well as to adults with careful attention, for example in school assembly, when they shared views on a parable for nearly half an hour. They are willing to 'have a go', and they predict, investigate and form hypotheses. All of this helps them to evaluate their own and others' work meaningfully and to present their ideas in a variety of ways.

[Overall: excellent attitudes (1)]

Example 2.2.2

Extracts from a Record of Corporate Judgements on a full inspection of a primary school

Strengths:	Sources of evidence:
• Youngest children are confident in the playground	• Evidence Forms (EFs) of playtime and lunchtimes Tuesday, Wednesday, Thursday
• Pupils in Y1, 3 and 5 behave well in lessons	• EFs EN/MA; HI in Y1; DT in Y3; PE in Y5
• Teachers in Y1, 3 and 5 model good behaviour	• EFs of lessons; discussions with pupils and parents' comments
• Little absenteeism	• EF of scrutiny of registers; PICSI data

Weaknesses:	Sources of evidence:
• Two incidents of racism observed in the playground	• EFs of am playtime and lunchtime Wednesday
• Racism was ignored by MSA and Y6 teacher	• EF of discussions between Asian boy and MSA teacher
• Inappropriate behaviour in lessons	• EF of Y1 EN lesson
• Rudeness to teacher	• EF of Y6 PE lesson
• Concerns about racism	• Parents' meeting
• Inconsistent approaches to discipline	• EFs from lessons and assemblies

Overall evaluation:

The approaches to managing behaviour are inconsistent. Behaviour is unsatisfactory overall. The school does not tackle the evident racism that exists.

REPORTING REQUIREMENTS

SUMMARY REPORT	In both FULL and SHORT INSPECTIONS complete the table PUPILS' ATTITUDES, VALUES AND PERSONAL DEVELOPMENT. Write brief evaluations about the strengths and weaknesses under the table.
	If any of these feature in the improvement of the school, record this in HOW THE SCHOOL HAS IMPROVED SINCE ITS LAST INSPECTION.
	Any aspects that are particularly good or need to improve should be reported under WHAT THE SCHOOL DOES WELL or WHAT COULD BE IMPROVED.
SHORT INSPECTIONS	If pupils' attitudes, values or personal development are either a strength of the school or a weakness they should become an area in the commentary.
FULL INSPECTIONS	Report in full under the heading PUPILS' ATTITUDES, VALUES AND PERSONAL DEVELOPMENT.

☐ **Pupils' attitudes to the school**

Are pupils keen and eager to come to school? Do they show interest in school life and are they involved in the range of activities the school provides?

Notice how children come into the school at the start of the day. See if they move around the school calmly and with purpose. Are they pleased to show you around and point out their own work as well as that of others? Pupils who are interested and involved will be keen to work in lessons, answer questions, engage with the task in hand, participate in the range of activities provided and show enthusiasm to get as much out of school as possible.

When pupils' attitudes to the school are good, consider the reasons why. These may include:

- good teaching and interesting lessons;

- pupils being clear about the way they should behave;

- successful links between home and school;

- how the school promotes the cultural traditions, aspirations and values pupils bring with them from home and their communities.

Consider the attitudes of different groups of pupils to the school, and, where there are differences, find out why. See if the school is aware of them and find out what is being done, if anything, about them.

☐ **Behaviour, including the incidence of exclusions**

Do pupils behave well in lessons and around the school, and are they courteous, trustworthy and respectful of the property of others?

Evaluate behaviour throughout the school day, in classrooms and when pupils are at play or lunch. Notice if pupils are polite to each other and to adults, and if they look after their own property as well as that of others. Look at the behaviour policy in the school, and find out if pupils contributed to it or know about it. Take account of the views expressed by parents either at the parents' meeting or in the questionnaires.

Exclusions are not common in primary schools but where they do occur you should follow them up to establish the reasons.

Example 2.2.3

> ***Extract from a full inspection report on a junior school***
>
> *Pupils behave well for most of the time. There are, however, isolated incidents of inappropriate behaviour usually involving a small group of 11-year-olds. These pupils joined the school recently and have not yet adjusted to the high expectations set by the school. The deputy headteacher meets daily with the pupils, and teachers send weekly behaviour reports, emphasising success as well as areas for improvement, to their parents. The steps taken by the school have been effective and have greatly reduced incidents of misbehaviour.*
>
> [Contributes to a judgement cf satisfactory behaviour (4)]

☐ Personal development and relationships

Do pupils show initiative and are they willing to take responsibility?

Find out if, for example, pupils:

- are involved in the daily routines of the school;

- notice what needs to be done and do it;

- help each other;

- when asked, are able to plan and organise their work;

- are more confident as they get older.

At different times, see whether pupils are given any opportunities to be responsible for the younger children. This may involve working with them, for example, in paired reading, helping to tidy up different activities or caring for plants or pets.

Example 2.2.4

> ***Extract from a short inspection report on a primary school***
>
> *Pupils willingly take a lot of responsibility in the classroom and the school. They run a very good 'buddy system' in which new pupils have a friend to look after them when they first join the school. They help them learn the school rules and look after them at lunch and playtimes. Older pupils are very confident in showing visitors round the school and give detailed explanations of what is happening in each class. The pupils are mature and have high regard for their teachers. They use their initiative well, anticipating what needs to be done, for example in setting up the hall for assembly without being asked.*
>
> [Contributes to a judgement of very good initiative and responsibility (2)]

Do pupils form constructive relationships with one another, and with teachers and other adults?

Most of the evidence about pupil and staff relationships and personal development will come from your observations of pupils around the school. Look for evidence of pupils working and playing well together, particularly those from different minority ethnic backgrounds. See how well they relate to staff and other adults in the school. Check if those with special educational needs are also included. Evaluate how well the pupils have learned to respect differences and understand the feelings, values and beliefs of others.

Do pupils reflect on and understand the impact of what they do on others? Do they respect the feelings, values and beliefs of others?

Very young children need to be helped by an adult to think about the results of their actions on others. Find ways to see if opportunities are given for this to happen.

As children get older their peers and others will help them understand how their actions make others feel. Observe how far pupils are able to listen to what others have to say and respond positively to ideas, views and feelings different from their own, and whether pupils understand and respect different values and beliefs.

Example 2.2.5

Extract from an* Inspection Notebook *for the full inspection of a primary school

- *When with adults, pupils are willing to be tolerant of others and accept adults' resolution of disagreements and conflicts. [S]*

- *When out of earshot of adults some pupils resort to name-calling and show a lack of tolerance and respect for others, particularly those who are different from themselves, for example the new group of refugee children. [W]*

[Contributes to a judgement of unsatisfactory behaviour (5)]

Do pupils work in an atmosphere free from oppressive behaviour, such as bullying, sexism and racism?

Nursery and reception children are particularly vulnerable, especially those with little or no English. They are easily frightened and intimidated by the loud or aggressive behaviour of older pupils or adults. Older children can also feel bullied and intimidated. Talk to children to find out if they know who to go to if they have a problem, and if they have a strategy to help them cope if they feel threatened.

Sexist and racist attitudes are formed very early; sometimes before children come to school. You need to assess how aware the adults in the school are of this and what steps they take to promote positive role models and counter negative attitudes throughout the school.

Example 2.2.6

Extract from a full inspection report on a first school

The teacher dealt sensitively and decisively when Y1 pupils in the role-play hospital strayed into stereotypical activities. She entered the play as a senior doctor and made some 'new staff appointments'. Her interventions challenged the view that 'boys couldn't be nurses'. She also made a note about the need to bring in a male nurse to talk about his work and to explore other areas, such as cooking, where stereotypical views might linger.

☐ **Attendance**

Are there high levels of attendance?

Attendance in primary schools is usually good. Use the data in the *PICSI report* to relate a school's attendance to the national picture. You need only make further inquiries if it is below 95 per cent or if you have concerns, for example about a downward trend. In this case, check how parents are asked to support the regular attendance of their children and if there are straightforward procedures for reporting absence. Check that registers are completed each morning and afternoon, and that they conform to the latest guidance. Look at the strategies the school uses in partnership with the Education Welfare Service to reduce the levels of unauthorised absence.

You should consider the school's own analysis of attendance data, especially if there are, for example, differences between year or ethnic groups. Does the school follow up absences? Does it compare its attendance with that of other schools?

3. HOW WELL ARE PUPILS TAUGHT?

Inspectors must evaluate and report on:

☐ the quality of teaching, judged in terms of its impact on pupils' learning and what makes it successful or not.

Inspectors must include evaluations of:

- how well the skills of literacy and numeracy are taught;

- how well the teaching meets the needs of all its pupils, taking account of age, gender, ethnicity, capability, special educational needs, gifted and talented, and those for whom English is an additional language;

- the teaching in each subject, commenting on any variations between subjects and year groups;

☐ how well pupils learn and make progress.

In determining their judgements, inspectors should consider the extent to which teachers:

- show good subject knowledge and understanding in the way they present and discuss their subject;

- are technically competent in teaching phonics and other basic skills;

- plan effectively, setting clear objectives that pupils understand;

- challenge and inspire pupils, expecting the most of them, so as to deepen their knowledge and understanding;

- use methods which enable all pupils to learn effectively;

- manage pupils well and insist on high standards of behaviour;

- use time, support staff and other resources, especially information and communications technology, effectively;

- assess pupils' work thoroughly and use assessments to help and encourage pupils to overcome difficulties;

- use homework effectively to reinforce and/or extend what is learned in school;

and the extent to which pupils:

- acquire new knowledge or skills, develop ideas and increase their understanding;

- apply intellectual, physical or creative effort in their work;

- are productive and work at a good pace;

- show interest in their work, are able to sustain concentration and think and learn for themselves;

- understand what they are doing, how well they have done and how they can improve.

INSPECTION FOCUS

Evaluation of the quality and impact of teaching is central to inspection. Teaching is fundamental to the quality of education provided by the school and the main avenue through which the school contributes to pupils' attainment, progress and attitudes. The effectiveness of teaching and the consequent rate, breadth, depth and consolidation of pupils' learning are intrinsically connected. It is the skill of rigorous and perceptive inspection to find, illustrate and evaluate the links between the two.

When evaluating the quality of teaching and learning in the school, the process of education, you should concentrate on these priorities:

■ evaluating the quality of teaching, in terms of how effective it is;

■ identifying which aspects of teaching work best, or least well;

■ recording and reporting these insights so as to illustrate good practice and to explain weaknesses clearly so as to provide a basis for improvement.

In every lesson observed, you should consider:

■ the subject matter, its context and relevance, and how it relates to the pupils and what they have done before;

■ the methods used and structure of the lesson, evaluating each of the lesson's components where these are distinct (as in a 'literacy hour');

■ the pupils, what they are required to do and how they do it, noticing the extent to which the lesson is engaging or addressing the needs of all of them as fully as it should.

In nursery and primary schools, teachers usually have responsibility for a class of pupils and for the teaching of that class. Often, particularly in nursery and reception classes, they are supported by teaching assistants, such as nursery nurses, whose work they direct. Often teachers and teaching support assistants work as a team. The latter make a valuable contribution to teaching and you should evaluate their contribution, providing feedback to support assistants in the way you do for teachers wherever possible. Final assessments of teaching, however, should only be provided for qualified teachers employed by the school. The work of teaching support staff however should feature in the teaching section of full reports.

TEACHING

Your insights stem from detailed classroom observation of teaching and pupils at work, complemented by the depth of understanding pupils show in discussion with you and your analysis of the quality and standards of the work they have done. This will enable you to see whether pupils are learning as much, as quickly and as well as you would expect, and to judge the quality of the teaching.

You need to explain your judgements by exemplifying what it is the teacher actually does that helps to make learning successful or not, and what could be done to improve it further. Do not become side-tracked in the pursuit of individual criteria at the expense of missing the key points in a lesson. Give particular attention to how well the skills of literacy and numeracy are taught and how well the needs of all pupils are met.

Judging teaching in subjects

In SHORT INSPECTIONS, judge the quality of teaching overall on the basis of all the lessons seen, and across subjects with an emphasis on observations of English and mathematics. When evaluating the quality of teaching of young children not yet working on the National Curriculum programmes of study, you need to assess the knowledge and competence of staff in the six areas of learning. In judging the teaching of pupils in Key Stages 1 and 2 you should focus particularly on the core subjects of English, mathematics, science and include information and communications technology, religious education (where it is being inspected) and a sample of lessons in other subjects.

On FULL INSPECTIONS abstract from your *Evidence Forms* to record your judgements about the teaching in the subjects that you are inspecting in your *Inspection Notebook*. Use the separate guidance on the inspection of subjects to identify the strengths and weaknesses of teaching in the subject at each Key Stage. You will need to bring these judgements to the team meetings to contribute to the judgement of the overall quality of teaching at each Key Stage and in the school as a whole.

Judging the overall quality of teaching in the school

Teaching overall is likely to be unsatisfactory if more than approximately one in ten lessons are so judged. If these contain poor or very poor teaching, or the proportion is higher than one in eight, you will need to consider whether the school has serious weaknesses. Once the proportion of unsatisfactory teaching reaches one lesson in five it is very likely to be in need of special measures. If almost all of the teaching in the school is good, with much of it very good or better, and there is no unsatisfactory teaching, the overall quality of teaching could be judged very good because of the consistently good or very good teaching.

Reporting on teaching in the school needs to be crystal clear in terms of its quality, what works, what does not, why and what should be done about it.

Make sure there is consistency between the messages you give on how well pupils are taught and the other two major areas of inspection: standards and the leadership and management of the school. Excellent leadership and management, for example, do not sit comfortably with teaching which is simply satisfactory with a few good lessons.

Judging the quality of teaching in lessons

The following characteristics illustrate where to pitch judgements about how well pupils are taught in lessons.

Very good or excellent	The teaching of skills and subject matter is knowledgeable, stimulating and perceptive. It uses imaginative resources and makes intellectual and creative demands on pupils to extend their learning. Challenging questions are used to consolidate, extend and verify what pupils know and understand. The methods chosen are well geared to the particular focus and demands of the lesson and make the most productive use of the time available. Relationships in the classroom provide a confident and positive atmosphere in which achievement flourishes. Pupils are keen to learn, rise to challenges in creative ways and think further. They work well for extended periods of time and make very good progress.
Satisfactory or better	The teaching of basic skills and subject content is clear and accurate, using clear explanation and demonstration, and involving all pupils. The organisation of the lesson allows most pupils to keep up with the work and to complete tasks in the time available. Staff interact with pupils to check their understanding and to ensure they remain on task. The relationship between the pupils and teacher is such that pupils can get on with their work and know how well they have done.

However, teaching **cannot be satisfactory** if any one of the following is present:

- the teacher's knowledge of the areas of learning or subjects is not good enough to promote demanding work;
- basic skills such as phonological awareness are not taught effectively;
- a significant minority of pupils are not engaged in the lesson;
- lessons are poorly planned and organised and time is wasted;
- there are weaknesses in controlling the class;
- pupils do not know what they are doing;
- pupils are not making much progress.

Example 3.1

Extract from an* Evidence Form *from a Y4 mathematics lesson starting with the whole class in a primary school

Mental arithmetic warm-up very challenging 'Think of a number, triple it, add five and take away two'. Excellent use of pupils' correct and incorrect answers. Highly perceptive questioning which enables individual calculation methods to be explored. Helps children overcome difficulties in understanding by saying 'Tell me how you got that answer'. Manages children very well and uses humour to good effect. Wide range of ability, activities tailored to the different ability groups in the class. Excellent explanation of digital route patterns and trends. Good follow-up homework set. Teaching well drawn from PoS. Newly qualified teacher!

[Overall: excellent teaching (1)]

Example 3.2

Extract from a **Record of Corporate Judgement** *from the short inspection of a primary school*

Strengths:

- *Learning objectives clear in planning particularly for LY and NY, very sharply defined for pupils of different abilities*

- *Children told at the beginning of lessons what and how they are expected to learn*

- *Good subject knowledge in English and mathematics (NB: Y2 EN very good illustration)*

- *Questions used effectively to check understanding, push thinking forward, assess next step in learning*

Sources of evidence:

- *EFs YR/Y1/Y2/Y5/Y6*

- *EFs recording discussion with Y6 re spelling and EFs for DT Y3, Gg Y4, AR Y6*

- *EFs EN MA all classes*

- *EFs SC Y1; RE Y2; EN Y4, 5 and 6, N YR*

Weaknesses:

- *High levels of noise making concentration difficult in some classes*

- *Marking varied, insufficient guidance to help pupils improve*

- *Learning activities not worthwhile*

- *Insufficient challenge for the most able*

Sources of evidence:

- *EF of Y5 MA; Y4, Y2, EN*

- *Scrutiny of work particularly evident in EN*

- *Y1 PE; EN pm session*

- *Y6 MA, Y5 EN, Y3 GG, Y2 DT*

Overall evaluation:

Strengths outweigh weaknesses and teaching is satisfactory overall. Good planning particularly in LY and NY but needs extending to challenge more able pupils. The clear objectives given to children are not used in assessing their work.

[Contributes to a judgement of satisfactory teaching (4)]

REPORTING REQUIREMENTS

SUMMARY REPORT

In both FULL and SHORT INSPECTIONS you must complete the table TEACHING AND LEARNING. In FULL INSPECTIONS, and where possible in SHORT INSPECTIONS, write brief comments about: the quality of teaching in English and mathematics; strengths and weaknesses in teaching; how well the school meets the needs of all pupils; the percentages of satisfactory or better, very good or better and unsatisfactory or worse teaching; and particular strengths and weaknesses in pupils' learning.

If any of these feature in the improvement of the school, report this in the section HOW THE SCHOOL HAS IMPROVED SINCE ITS LAST INSPECTION.

If any aspects of teaching are particularly good or need to improve you must report these under WHAT THE SCHOOL DOES WELL or WHAT COULD BE IMPROVED.

SHORT INSPECTIONS

In the commentary, expand your judgements on teaching as reported either in WHAT THE SCHOOL DOES WELL or WHAT COULD BE IMPROVED. Complete the data tables in Part C of the report, including the data on teaching.

FULL INSPECTIONS

Report fully under the heading HOW WELL ARE PUPILS TAUGHT? Complete the data tables in Part C of the report, including the data on teaching.

GUIDANCE ON USING THE CRITERIA

In order to stress the importance of evaluating teaching through its impact, this guidance puts learning first. The criteria for learning are encapsulated in the questions: to what extent are the pupils engaged? challenged? extended? For teaching, the questions include: are pupils taught the right things in an effective manner and at the right pace?

☐ How well pupils learn and make progress

Do pupils acquire new knowledge or skills, develop ideas and increase their understanding?

In forming your judgements about the acquisition of knowledge, skills or understanding, take every opportunity to relate this to the work done previously. Learning may be consolidated or may cover new ground in the lesson you observe. Your judgements should, where possible, be referenced to what has gone before. The learning objectives identified by the teacher will help you to ask pupils relevant questions and to judge whether the teaching and learning are well matched to the pupils' age and capability. Whenever you can, record specific examples of how the teaching helps the pupils to understand more.

Examination of pupils' work and discussion with them will also help you to decide if the work in hand is building on pupils' current knowledge, understanding or skills. When you analyse samples of work, focus on evidence of progress over a period of time, and within the same year group. Look for consistency of approach and content between classes covering the same age range. The analysis of work, recorded on *Evidence Forms*, should provide detailed information about the rate, quantity and quality of pupils' learning, not simply a list of the content covered over time (*see Example 3.3*).

Discussion with pupils about what they are doing can give you an insight into how they acquire new knowledge and skills, and increase their understanding across the subjects of the curriculum. On SHORT INSPECTIONS, this may be your prime source of evidence of work in some subjects.

Example 3.3

Evidence Form *recording the analysis of pupils' written work in English in an infant school*

Context:

Work from autumn and summer terms. Work of six children, two above average (AA),
two average (A), two below average (BA) from two parallel classes 2YE and 2YA.

Teaching:

Work indicates that all pupils, except those with a statement, have covered the same range of work.
Teaching shows coverage of PoS and, this term's attention to NLS Framework. Work in Y2E is regularly
marked and includes comments to help the pupils to progress and to improve. Sheet in the front of each
book reminds pupils of the drafting process, spelling strategies and personal targets for the term.
Work shows they are mindful of the teachers' expectations. In the parallel class Y2A, pupils have been
taught by a succession of teachers, and now have NQT in post for only six weeks. (Management issue
co-ordinator/headteacher not given the NQT guidelines for marking English work.)

Pupils' standards:

In autumn, AA were working at Level 2 (short sentences; accurate use of capital letters and full stops;
continuous narrative; address separate from letter; letters formed evenly and accurately; spelling of
words with common letter strings secure) and are now reaching L3 (different forms of writing such as
reports and poetry; careful choice of adjectives; appropriate use of ! ?; fluent cursive writing; very good
attempts to spell polysyllabic words). Steady progress in writing not as good as expected for AA pupils;
slight dip in quality and quantity of work during spring term.

In autumn, A pupils were working towards L2. Letter writing showed use of caps and full stops slightly
less reliably than the AA stories but have clear structure and writing well formed. Covered the same
range of work as the AAs and made less progress. Now use capital letters and full stops confidently but do
not use other forms of punctuation. Adjectives limited to the more mundane, e.g., 'nice', 'good'. Writing
joined but hesitant and uneven; spell words with common letter strings accurately but confuse
homonyms. Gains over the year less than one would have expected; standards only just maintained.
Work recorded in books in spring term of poor quality; much incomplete. (Confirms concerns raised by
parents about the impact of several changes of teacher.) Pupils have made up lost ground this term.
Overall, progress just satisfactory.

Work of BA pupils' variations in progress marked. Autumn term barely writing. Much of recorded work
is teacher scribed. Few words written independently, poorly formed and barely legible. Worksheets show
gaps in phonemic awareness. Spring term pupils completed nothing but worksheets on initial sounds.
(All correct but nothing to show how well this understood or applied.) Current term writing has
progressed at an impressive rate. (Recently appointed part-time specialist teacher working with these
pupils during group work in literacy hour has had a significant impact on standards and progress.)
The pupils are achieving as well as the As. There is no discernible difference in the quality or the
quantity of their work. Progress poor during the early part of the year but very good in recent times.
Standards and progress reflect the quality of teaching.

Learning:	Attainment:
AA sample – satisfactory	AA sample – satisfactory
A sample – unsatisfactory	A sample – satisfactory
BA sample – good	BA sample – good

Do pupils apply intellectual, physical or creative effort in their work and are they working productively and at a good pace?

Most pupils will make an effort in their work if the teaching makes demands and provides the encouragement which enables them to do so. You need to judge, therefore, the extent to which pupils are engaged in their work, whether the effort involved is enough or too much, and whether it was worthwhile in relation to what has been learnt. Every lesson should contribute in some way towards the pupils' development or consolidation of knowledge, skills or understanding. The pupils should be able to explain what they are doing and have done, and what they have learnt at the end of each session. Pupils are far more likely to apply effort in their work when they see why they are working in a particular way, and what they are required to understand is important.

The amount of work pupils do, the extent to which they have to concentrate, and their attitude to the task, will indicate if they are working to capacity. Pupils do not always work at a good pace unless the teacher expects them to. During lesson observations try to return to the same pupils more than once to judge if they are working well enough and getting through the required amount of work. This also provides evidence of the teacher's use of time. Good teaching routines encourage pupils to manage their own time well and to get through what is required in the time available.

Do pupils show interest in their work? Are they able to sustain concentration and thinking and learn for themselves? Do pupils understand what they are doing, how well they have done and how they can improve?

Pupils are likely to show interest and understanding when the explanations, tasks, activities and challenges presented are lively and interesting. Effective teachers constantly relate new learning to old, encouraging pupils to make the links between areas of learning and to think imaginatively for themselves.

Successful teachers make clear to the pupils what they are expected to learn, the standards that are expected, and how they can do even better next time. For very young children in a nursery class, the teacher has to make this explicit for the children. Older pupils in primary schools can frequently be expected to be much more independent. For example, deciding as a group what they think will be good enough and how they might improve their own work and the work of others.

Example 3.4

Extract from an **Evidence Form** *recording a Y1 information technology lesson with pupils working in pairs on computers*

All show clear understanding of the routines and procedures involved in loading and using software. Progress evident in improved control of the mouse and in discussion using words such as 'keyboard' and 'icon'. Some of the pairs were discussing how they could improve their picture next time. All were keen to do well. When errors were made by using a single blue line to create sky, they evaluated the aesthetic effect for themselves and worked together to find another way (e.g., a rectangular box coloured blue).

[Overall: very good learning (2)]

To summarise, you can expect learning to be effective when the teaching is good. The pupils will be keen and interested from the beginning of the lesson. They are clear about what they are doing and why they are doing it. They can see the links with their earlier learning and have some ideas about how it then could be developed further. The pupils want to know more and take responsibility for finding out more of their own accord. They understand what is good about their work and how it can be improved. They support one another and know when and where to go for help.

☐ **The quality of teaching, judged in terms of its impact on pupils' learning and what makes it successful or not**

Do teachers show good subject knowledge and understanding in the way they present and discuss their subject?

Evaluate the success of teaching and what makes it so. For teachers of young children, who have not yet embarked on the National Curriculum programmes of study, their 'subject knowledge' is what they know and understand about the content of the Early Learning Goals and of how children develop. You can judge teachers' subject knowledge by observing, for example:

- how competently they teach the content of the Early Learning Goals, National Curriculum programmes of study and the RE syllabus;

- how competently they plan the area of work and learning in the subject or show a good understanding of the way the subject develops;

- how well they teach the skills of literacy and numeracy;

- their skills in asking subject specific questions which help pupils to understand and which extend their thinking;

- how well they explain new ideas in a way that make sense to pupils;

- how well they draw on their knowledge of how children learn when presenting them with new experiences or information;

- how well they use equipment, artefacts and resources to interest and challenge the pupils;

- their ability to deepen the thinking in the subject for all pupils and stretch the more able.

Are teachers technically competent in teaching phonics and other basic skills?

TEACHING LITERACY

The National Literacy Strategy, including the literacy hour, is non-statutory and some schools may have alternative approaches designed to improve standards in reading and writing. You must form a view about the effectiveness of the school's strategy for literacy, the quality of teaching, and the standards achieved. Some entire literacy lessons must be observed.

Very good teachers of literacy skills combine competence in the full range of technical knowledge with the flair to put it across in ways that make language come alive for children.

When completing *Evidence Forms* evaluate each of the components of the literacy hour observed. When evaluating literacy you should look for:

- thorough knowledge of the National Literacy Strategy (NLS) Framework for teaching;

- secure understanding of the literacy skills to be taught;

- secure knowledge and understanding of the literacy skills which pupils need;

- good understanding of how to teach phonics, including phonological awareness, the blending of sounds in words for reading, segmenting words into sounds for spelling, and a knowledge of spelling rules;

- good use of the NLS teaching objectives in short- and medium-term planning;

- balance between word, sentence and text-level work.

Example 3.5

Extract from Evidence Form *recording a Y2 literacy lesson – autumn term programme*

Context:

Literacy hour – whole class shared text work and word-level work.

Work on words: vowel phonemes 'ow' and 'ou'; work on sentences: revise reading of ! and ?; work on text: Shirley Hughes' poem 'Grasshouse'. Plenary: checking on learning.

Evidence:

Pupils told what they would be doing in the lesson and what they were expected to learn. Effective questioning to revise previous work. What did we say were the main differences between a poem and a story? CA assessed and recorded pupils' responses. New poem, written on the white board with several words covered by strips of paper. Read first two lines giving more emphasis to punctuation. Pupils challenged to think what the first covered word might be. Eager to suggest ideas. Good contribution to progress in reading. Pupils expected to give good reasons for their final choice . . . 'it makes sense, it rhymes with the last word on the next line but one'. Word revealed 'house' introduced vowel phoneme 'ou'. Explained well; good phonemic awareness, helped pupils to self-correct when suggestions were not accurate. Pupils eager to suggest rhyming words. 'Cow' led easily to 'ow'. Familiar words listed. By the end of the word-level work all pupils could read the poem and knew how to spell and read words such as 'house' and 'owl'. Plenary well focused on what had been learned.

[Overall: good teaching (3)]

For pupils of 5 and under in nursery and reception classes, focus on how well the teacher develops children's awareness and understanding of language and literacy skills needed to read and write. Evaluate how well children are learning through their talk, and the extent to which the teaching builds on children's own language to develop their knowledge of letters, sounds and words, and their ability to read and write.

The teaching of literacy is most effective when reading and writing build on speaking and listening, and pupils are excited about language and the power of story. You need to judge how this develops for pupils of different ages as they use language with more skill and come to understand why literacy is important. Judge whether or not all pupils, throughout the school, speak, listen and use language to good effect.

Teaching numeracy within the dedicated mathematics lesson

The *National Numeracy Strategy: Framework for Teaching Mathematics* has been introduced for primary schools, and complements the National Literacy Strategy. You must form a view about the impact of the school's strategy for numeracy on the quality of teaching and the standards achieved. When completing *Evidence Forms* evaluate each component of the daily lesson for mathematics. Some complete mathematics lessons should be seen. When evaluating numeracy you should look at:

- the quality of teachers' plans – whether the school makes good use of the objectives listed in the numeracy Framework to establish progression in pupils' learning;

- the extent to which pupils are informed about the learning objectives, the mathematical skills and knowledge they are to learn, what they are to do, how long it should take and the progress they are making;

- how effectively the teacher's introduction to the mathematics lesson engages all pupils, sets a brisk pace, and encourages and enables pupils to participate in oral and mental work, by giving them appropriate thinking time, promoting quick recall skills and efficient mental calculation strategies;

- the teacher's and pupils' correct use of mathematical vocabulary and notation, providing the language for pupils to explain their thinking, solutions and strategies, and helping pupils to interpret and make accurate use of words and symbols;

- how well the teacher explains, demonstrates and illustrates the mathematics being taught – drawing on the class for ideas, solutions, methods and practical contributions, using well-focused questions which provide opportunities to check pupils' understanding, to correct any mistakes, and employ resources to establish mathematical relationships or properties that assist in communication between the teacher and pupils;

- whether the activities pupils are engaged in are appropriately matched to the intended learning objectives and are suitably adapted to meet the learning needs of pupils within different ability groups;

- how effectively the lesson is concluded, whether the teacher highlights: the key facts, ideas and vocabulary pupils have learned and need to remember; identifies what has been achieved; looks forward to the next lesson and sets any out-of-class work or homework to consolidate or extend the mathematics in the lesson;

- teachers' knowledge of mathematics and of the mathematics curriculum – whether teachers make appropriate use of the Framework's objectives and examples to help to identify progression over time and the methods of calculation that pupils are to be taught, are quick to recognise pupils' mistakes and use these as teaching points, and can identify key ideas in mathematics and relationships between topics.

Example 3.6

Extract from an Evidence Form *observing a numeracy lesson in a Y1/2/3 class organised into five groups in a small primary school*

Evidence:

Teacher uses a good range of mathematical and everyday language to introduce concept of multiplication to one group, e.g., 'sets, groups, piles'. Explains clearly what multiplication means, checking understanding by asking questions of individuals. She offers encouragement to children to come up with the solutions themselves. An effective eye is kept on the other groups, but children know what is expected and get on with it. Teacher questioning also effectively used to test recall of number bonds addition. Multiplication activity extends the range of calculation strategies children can use and effectively moves from handling materials practically to mental and written work. The resources (mostly teacher-made sheets) are differentiated. The pace was good for the x group, moving in 45 minutes from simple introduction with cubes to x tables.

[Overall: very good teaching (2)]

Do teachers plan effectively, setting clear objectives that pupils understand?

In a lesson, session or sequence of lessons, look for clear objectives for what pupils are to learn and how these objectives will be achieved. Does planning take into account the differing needs of pupils, such as those with specific difficulties? Whatever form the planning takes, look for evidence of what teachers intend and how they will know if their intentions are met. Once you know what the lesson aims to do, you can ask relevant questions when you talk to the pupils and make accurate judgements about the success or otherwise of the lesson.

If there is time, discuss with teachers how the lesson fits into the teacher's longer-term plans and why, for example, they use particular methods. Such discussions provide insight into teachers' planning and their response to changing situations, which are not always recorded on paper.

Consider how support staff are involved in planning the teaching and how they are briefed about what they are expected to do. This is particularly important in nursery classes where nursery nurses often work jointly with the class teacher in setting the learning objectives and planning the work.

Do teachers challenge and inspire pupils, expecting the most of them, so as to deepen their knowledge and understanding?

You may see lessons where teachers advance learning in an atmosphere of imaginative speculation and curiosity, unconstrained by subject boundaries. They provide pointers to new connections and deeper understanding, provoking determined and unexpected contribution from pupils. The challenge lies in the intellectual and imaginative effort needed; the inspiration in the new directions the pupils take. Few teachers can manage this all the time but you should be quick to recognise it and praise it when you see it.

Do teachers use methods which enable all pupils to learn effectively?

Consider how well teachers match the methods they use to the purpose of the lesson. The key to the judgements you make is whether these methods and their organisation are likely to result in high standards of work and behaviour for all pupils. If there are any pupils, or groups of pupils, who are not involved and not learning effectively, then you must find out the reasons for this. Consider specifically whether the methods used support pupils of high ability, those with special educational needs and, where relevant, pupils for whom English is an additional language.

You will need to evaluate whether:

- the teacher's exposition or explanation is lively, informative and well structured;

- any grouping by ability promotes higher standards;

- the teacher's use and style of questioning probe pupils' knowledge and understanding, challenge their thinking and engage all pupils;

- practical activity is purposeful and not stereotyped in that pupils are encouraged to think about what they are doing, what they have learned from it and how to improve their work;

- investigations and problem-solving activities help pupils to apply and extend their learning in new contexts;

- the choice of pupil grouping, for example pupils working alone, in pairs or small groups or all together, achieves the objectives for teaching and learning;

- the form of organisation allows the teacher to interact efficiently with as many pupils as possible;

- the use of resources stimulates learning and sensitively reflects different groups, cultures and backgrounds.

The choice of teaching methods is a matter for the school. You must judge whether what is done is effective.

Do teachers manage pupils well and insist on high standards of behaviour?

You should consider the quality of relationships in the classroom and the extent to which teachers create a purposeful working atmosphere.

Some important features, which reduce the incidence of inappropriate behaviour, include the extent to which:

- the teacher exercises authority clearly and fairly from the outset;

- the teacher holds the pupils' attention and involves them in the work in hand, encouraging their concentration and completion of the task;

- the organisation of the work to be done and the grouping of pupils to do it are carried out clearly and efficiently;

- the teacher supports and controls the pupils, intervening according to the needs of individuals and groups;

- there is mutual respect between teacher and pupils and proper habits of work are established and developed;

- the teacher stresses the importance of self-discipline and has expectations of mature behaviour.

Do teachers use time, support staff and other resources, especially information and communications technology (ICT), effectively?

Management of the pupils, time, resources and support promotes good behaviour and effective learning. Resources should be sufficient in quantity and quality, and fitted to the intended work.

Central to your judgements relating to these criteria is the extent to which teachers manage time and resources so that pupils work productively. In effective lessons the pace is usually brisk, but there are occasions when time is needed for reflection and consolidation.

Evaluate whether teachers use time efficiently and whether pupils know what they have to do and how long they have in which to do it.

During Key Stage 1 pupils should be taught to:

- use ICT tools with confidence;

- become familiar with different hardware and software;

- compose and develop their ideas;

- increase their use of ICT-based information in other areas of work;

- amend material for others to read and use.

As you evaluate the work of teachers in teaching IT capability, check to see that it centres upon the teacher's expectation of pupils in their use of resources and their development or consolidation of knowledge. In primary schools, pupils will often be working independently or in pairs when using ICT tools and the teacher will frequently be engaged in other activities with the class. You need to observe the pupils and the way the teacher interacts with them to find out if there is a clearly understood expectation of what the pupils should be doing and why. The activity may be planned to develop IT capability, support learning within the subject or both. How effectively teachers use ICT tools is dependent upon the clarity of their intention and the quality of intervention and support given during the use of ICT. You need to judge whether the teacher's intervention merely solves technical problems or maintains pupils' attention upon the task. Does it enhance pupils' understanding of IT, the subject or both? When parents or support staff are directed by the teacher to help pupils using ICT, they too need to be aware of what the teacher expects from the use of the ICT and what they should do to ensure the intended learning takes place.

Example 3.7

Extract from Evidence Form *recording a Y5 history lesson using ICT in a primary school*

Focus for first session is exploring layouts and web pages for info on Ancient Rome. Challenging open-ended tasks given to pairs, e.g., 'You have five minutes to find out how you can move and change pictures, text and layout boxes.' Followed instructions well and shared good understanding of terms such as 'clip art', 'layout', 'enlarging' and 'reducing'.

Pupils quickly moved to accessing the Net for information on Romans in Britain. Knew quickly if it was relevant or not by applying what they already knew, e.g., 'Rome won't be any good, it will be about holidays, we want Ancient Rome.' Good levels of attainment in handling information and controlling tasks. Clear understanding of how this ICT knowledge will be used to support their history topic.

[Overall: good teaching and learning (3)]

Do teachers assess pupils' work thoroughly and use assessments to help and encourage pupils to overcome difficulties?

Your judgements about teachers' assessment of their pupils should focus on how well teachers look for gains in learning, gaps in knowledge and areas of misunderstanding, through their day-to-day work with pupils. This will include marking, questioning of individuals and plenary sessions. Clues to the effectiveness of formative assessment are how well the teachers listen and respond to pupils, encourage and, where appropriate, praise them, recognise and handle misconceptions, build on their responses and steer them towards clearer understanding. Effective teachers encourage pupils to judge the success of their own work and set targets for improvement. They will take full account of the targets set out in individual education plans for pupils with special educational needs.

Do teachers use homework effectively to reinforce and/or extend what is learned in school?

When judging how well teachers make use of homework find out the school's policy for homework and establish whether homework:

■ is planned to integrate with classwork;

■ is tailored to individual learning needs;

■ helps pupils to learn independently;

■ is regularly and constructively marked.

You should also establish whether parents understand how to help pupils with their homework.

How well does the teaching meet the needs of all pupils?

In this *Handbook* references have been made to the importance of evaluating the effectiveness of teaching and learning for all pupils. As an inspector, your thinking about the needs of all pupils and ensuring equal opportunities is not an optional extra but an integral aspect of the judgements you make about teaching, as it is for the other sections of the inspection schedule.

In coming to judgements about how well teachers promote and provide for equal opportunities, you will need to assess whether or not the teaching methods, the access to resources, and the time of day or year, disadvantage any groups of pupils, for example, if pupils were absent from school to celebrate Eid. You will also need to take account of pupils' ages, gender, ethnicity and capability on reaching your conclusions. For example, the choice of texts for the literacy hour might favour girls; pupils may be regularly withdrawn from mathematics in order to practise reading skills or for instrumental music tuition; the religious background of the pupils prevents them from taking part in activities which promote their spiritual or cultural development; or unavoidable lateness to school may result in a pupil always missing the introduction to work in science.

Example 3.8

Extract from an inspection report focusing on the teaching of pupils from minority ethnic backgrounds

Traveller children receive good-quality teaching from the Traveller Learning Support Assistant (TLSA). This ensures that these pupils make good progress in their lessons. Long-term plans and lesson activities are agreed with class teachers to ensure that work is well matched to the needs of individual pupils enabling learning to be consolidated when support is not available. Teachers have a good understanding of the Travellers' culture and they value and build on the experiences these pupils bring to the school. Although many of the pupils are in the school for less than one term they return annually. The school maintains good records of previous work. Teachers are quick to assess returning pupils and take account of all they have done since the previous year. Learning is very effective because pupils are well motivated by the tasks teachers prepare. They are clear what has to be done and teachers value their work.

You will need to pay particular attention to the school's provision for three particular groups of pupils: those with special educational needs; those who have English as an additional language; gifted and talented pupils.

How well does the school meet the needs of pupils with special educational needs (SEN)?

When judging how well the teaching meets the needs of pupils with special education needs, look for its impact on the learning of pupils on the register of special educational needs. The class teacher's plans for pupils should ensure that the work is matched to pupils' needs and show how the pupils are making progress. The effectiveness of planning is important because it enables the SEN co-ordinator, or LEA SEN support staff, to liaise successfully with class teachers, whether the pupils are supported in class or are withdrawn from lessons. Check to see that individual education plans (IEPs) contain clear targets and are sufficiently practical for class teachers to implement when support staff are not present.

You will also need to judge the effectiveness of any learning support assistants in providing the right blend of help and challenge, so that pupils do not become too dependent. Record your observations on the gains pupils make towards the targets set and, whenever possible, exemplify the achievements of pupils with particular disabilities. Make sure your judgements are consistent with those you record in HOW HIGH ARE STANDARDS? about the progress pupils make, and with what you report in the summary.

Example 3.9

> **Extract from an Evidence Form of mathematics lesson with a Y3 class containing several pupils with special educational needs**
>
> *Teacher's notes show very carefully planned lesson, good short-term achievable targets, work differentiated appropriately for different attainments. Work for pupils with SEN matches number targets in IEPs well. Good revision of previous learning. Listen attentively, keep involved and offer alternative ways of working. Expectations set and the teacher recorded the agreed target on board 'To work quietly and quickly to find the easiest ways to calculate our answers'. Settle quickly to individual tasks, often discuss freely with neighbour. Very well prepared. Lower-attaining pupils select a calculator to help them with tables. Traveller Learning Support Assistant (TLSA) worked with two pupils and a simple worksheet was completed. Good LSA support for statemented pupil with dyspraxia. Skilful management strategies focus well on pupils with SEN. Good emphasis on mathematical language. Positive approach, gives praise. Very good evaluation of work at the end of the lesson.*
>
> [Overall: very good teaching (2)]

How well does the school meet the needs of pupils with English as an additional language?

You will need to evaluate whether the planning and teaching methods take account of the language and learning needs of pupils with English as an additional language (EAL). This involves the identification of those who need additional support; not just when they are in the early stages of learning English, but also those at more advanced levels whose literacy skills often fail to do justice to their academic potential. Giving appropriate support will consist of some or all of the following:

- ensuring pupils have opportunities for supported speaking and listening;
- providing effective models of spoken and written language (for example, through 'writing frames');
- understanding how the first language can be used to support the learning of a second;
- using high-quality, culturally relevant visual aids and other resources;
- providing bilingual support assistants.

In inspecting EAL, you should look to see whether all the work is firmly placed within the National Curriculum. Withdrawal of pupils from lessons should be kept to a minimum, and their teaching needs to contain the same features as those outlined above.

How well does the school meet the needs of gifted and talented pupils?

To reach their full potential, gifted and talented pupils need challenging tasks that stretch them intellectually. You need to explore:

- how the school identifies its gifted and talented pupils;
- the awareness of staff of these pupils;
- the willingness of teachers to adapt and adjust to take account of pupils' rapid development;
- the school's strategies for ensuring that all teachers are able to share in providing the level of subject support needed;
- how the school draws on sources of support for gifted and talented pupils.

4. HOW GOOD ARE THE CURRICULAR AND OTHER OPPORTUNITIES OFFERED TO PUPILS?

Inspectors must evaluate and report on:

☐ the quality and range of opportunities for learning provided by the school for all pupils, highlighting features which are particular strengths and weaknesses;

---

including specific comment on:

- **extra-curricular activities** including study support;

- **the provision made for personal, social and health education,** including sex education and attention to drug misuse;

- **the quality of links with the community and with other schools, colleges or initial teacher training consortia;**

☐ whether the school meets statutory curricular requirements, including provision of religious education where appropriate;

☐ how well the school cultivates pupils' personal – including spiritual, moral, social and cultural – development.

In determining their judgements, inspectors should consider the extent to which the school:

- provides a broad range of worthwhile opportunities which meet the interests, aptitudes and particular needs of pupils, including those having special educational needs;

- has effective strategies for teaching the basic skills of literacy and numeracy;

- provides enrichment through its extra-curricular provision, including support for learning outside the school day;

- is socially inclusive by ensuring equality of access and opportunity for all pupils;

- provides pupils with the knowledge and insights into values and beliefs, and enables them to reflect on their experiences in a way which develops their spiritual awareness and self-knowledge;

- promotes principles which distinguish right from wrong;

- encourages pupils to take responsibility, show initiative and develop an understanding of living in a community;

- teaches pupils to appreciate their own cultural traditions and the diversity and richness of other cultures;

- provides effectively for personal and social education, including health education, sex education and attention to drug misuse;

- has links with the community which contribute to pupils' learning;

- has constructive relationships with partner institutions such as link schools.

INSPECTION FOCUS

You should evaluate the extent to which the content and organisation of the curriculum provide access to the full range of learning experiences and promote the high achievement and personal development of all pupils. The curriculum comprises all the planned activities within and beyond the school day.

The school should meet all it is required to by statute in Key Stages 1 and 2, and the beginning of Key Stage 3 for middle-deemed-primary schools. That is, it should meet National Curriculum requirements in the core subjects of English, mathematics, science, the other foundation subjects and, where it applies, the locally agreed syllabus requirements for religious education.

You will need to refer to the appropriate section in *Form S3,* the school self-audit, to gauge the school's perception of how far it meets statutory curriculum requirements. Your analysis of the information from these sources should enable you to raise pertinent questions with the school and to focus on areas which may need to be followed up during the inspection. If everything is in order and the school has made its provision on the basis of what is right for its pupils, then do not waste time looking further. You should only pursue further evidence if you suspect there is a significant problem in terms of what the pupils are entitled to receive, or if there is an area or subject of the curriculum that is particularly good.

Effective schools help pupils to become confident people with enduring values, able to contribute effectively to society. The experiences offered are rich and stimulating, contributing to the personal development of all individuals, and so helping them prepare for life as adults.

In your assessment of the opportunities offered to pupils you should find out what the school is really good at. Take note of any areas of excellence, for example in art, music or sport. The good school will ensure that the quality and range of opportunities for learning cover all the key aspects of personal development, with an emphasis on provision for **spiritual, moral social and cultural development**.

Within the framework of 'best value' (*see Annex 1*), the principle of 'challenge' means that the school should know why its curriculum has been planned as it has. Part of your work is to explore this; in particular, how the school has arrived at the balance of the statutory to the non-statutory curriculum, and how the school checks that it is providing what parents want when, for example, providing a modern foreign language in the primary school.

The curriculum in nursery schools or classes and reception classes should cover the following areas of learning: personal, social and emotional development; language and literacy; mathematics; knowledge and understanding of the world; physical development; and creative development. This curriculum should emphasise personal, social and emotional development, language and literacy and mathematics. The approach should be through talk, enquiry and play, with the aim of developing positive attitudes to learning.

The evidence you gather will be common to all inspections; however, in SHORT INSPECTIONS you are only required to make judgements and report on the three sections that relate to the quality and range of the curriculum, to the statutory requirements, and to pupils' personal development.

A wide range of evidence contributes to the evaluation of the curriculum. Before the inspection, refer to *Forms S2* and *S3* to gauge the school's perception of how far it meets the statutory curriculum requirements and the DfEE recommendations for 'taught time' for each Key Stage. If the taught time falls below the recommended minimum, you must report this. Form an impression of the quality of what the school offers through your reading of the prospectus and other documents. This impression will be reinforced or rejected once you begin gathering evidence in the school.

In SHORT INSPECTIONS, extensive evaluation of curriculum provision is neither possible nor desirable, but must include whether or not it meets statutory requirements and how well it provides for the spiritual, moral, social and cultural development of pupils.

The following characteristics illustrate where to pitch judgements about the quality of the curriculum.

Very good or excellent	The curriculum interprets statutory requirements in stimulating, as well as structured ways, providing for high achievement, particularly in core subjects, and offering pupils a wealth of additional opportunities. It uses resources from within and outside the school very effectively to enrich the curriculum. High priority is given to developing pupils' facility in the basic skills across subjects. Pupils' personal development is promoted through opportunities for pupils to take significant responsibility and initiative. Pupils clearly understand what is right and wrong, and show a high degree of respect for the differences between people and for their values and beliefs. The curriculum draws positively on their own cultural, family and religious backgrounds.
Satisfactory or better	The curriculum meets the statutory requirements, including those for children aged 5 and under, and takes account of the National Strategies for literacy and numeracy. Some additional activities are provided which are suitable for children of different ages and needs. Reasonable use is made of resources within the community; visits and other activities are planned to contribute to pupils' learning. Some opportunities for responsibility and initiative are provided. Pupils understand the difference between right and wrong, and respect the traditions, values and beliefs of others.

However, the curriculum **cannot be satisfactory** if:

- statutory requirements, including any significant aspects of the core subjects, are not met, and/or;

- it takes little or no account of the National Strategies for literacy and numeracy, especially where standards of literacy and numeracy are not high enough;

- it does little to inculcate respect, tolerance and good behaviour;

- it is unduly narrow in opportunities for personal development or curricular enrichment.

Example 4.1

Extract from a nursery school inspection report

The school provides a wide range of stimulating learning activities both in and out of doors for its children. An example was the area set up as an airport and aeroplane, where children 'check in' and 'travel' on a plane. The well-planned curriculum covers all the national Early Learning Goals. Both teachers and nursery nurses take an active part in planning and developing the curriculum, and build into it the role of volunteer helpers, which includes many parents. Staff are fully aware of the children with particular needs. For example, when a group of children were exploring the contents of a 'feely bag' the nursery nurse adapted her questions to match the different levels of the children's use of language. Teachers create too few opportunities for children to talk about what they are doing, however, and this detracts from the standards they could achieve in language and literacy.

[Contributes to a judgement that the curriculum is satisfactory (4)]

Example 4.2

Extract from a Record of Corporate Judgements *in the full inspection of a primary school*

Strengths:	**Sources of evidence:**
• *KS1 fully meets statutory requirements much of high quality*	• *EFs on curriculum analysis; discussions with HT and co-ordinators*
• *EN and MA well planned building in LY NY effectively both Key Stages*	• *EFs from Y2, Y6, Y3 EFs from co-ordinator*
• *Broad range of extra-curricular activities*	• *EF JS12*

Weaknesses:	**Sources of evidence:**
• *KS2 time allocation does not meet DfEE minimum*	• *Form S2; discussion with HT*
• *Emphasis on EN and MA at KS2 squeezed time for SC which is not sufficient to cover the NC*	• *EF interview with SC co-ordinator; scrutiny of work EFs of SC lessons*
• *IT in KS2 only included communicating information*	• *EF on analysis of ICT policy*

Overall evaluation:

School does not meet statutory requirements for NC in KS2 in science and ICT because too little time is provided for KS2 curriculum.

[Contributes to judgements of a good curriculum at KS1 (3) and a poor one at KS2 (6)]

REPORTING REQUIREMENTS

SUMMARY REPORT	In all inspections, the first boxes of the table headed OTHER ASPECTS OF THE SCHOOL must be completed, with comment on particular strengths and weaknesses, and any areas that do not meet statutory requirements.
	If any of these are a feature of improvement in the school, report this in the section HOW THE SCHOOL HAS IMPROVED SINCE ITS LAST INSPECTION.
	Any aspects that are particularly good or need to improve should be reported under WHAT THE SCHOOL DOES WELL and WHAT COULD BE IMPROVED.
SHORT INSPECTIONS	Expand your judgements in the commentary on matters listed in WHAT THE SCHOOL DOES WELL or WHAT COULD BE IMPROVED.
FULL INSPECTIONS	Report on overall quality and, particularly, on curricular strengths and weaknesses under the heading HOW GOOD ARE THE CURRICULAR AND OTHER OPPORTUNITIES OFFERED TO PUPILS?

GUIDANCE ON USING THE CRITERIA

☐ The quality and range of opportunities for learning provided by the school for all pupils, highlighting features which are particular strengths and weaknesses

☐ Whether the school meets statutory requirements, including provision of religious education where appropriate

Does the school provide a broad range of worthwhile opportunities which meet the interests, aptitudes and special needs of pupils, including those having special educational needs?

Before the inspection you should refer to *Form S3* to check whether or not the school is meeting the statutory requirements for the curriculum. Section D2 of *Form S2* will enable you to evaluate how the school allocates the time available to the different subjects of the curriculum. Your evaluation of the breadth and quality of the provision requires you to consider how the school has made decisions about what will be included in the curriculum, and the time allocated to different aspects, taking account of:

■ the programmes of study of the National Curriculum and the Early Learning Goals;

■ the importance of literacy and numeracy;

■ the current guidance from the Qualifications and Curriculum Authority (QCA);

■ the needs of all pupils;

■ the best use of the specialist skills of staff;

■ the organisation of the school day;

■ how the school ensures the needs of all pupils are met and that they have equal access to all areas of the curriculum and opportunities to succeed in them.

Displays can give a first impression of standards of work in some subjects. Look for displays which cover a broad range of the subjects of the curriculum and other aspects of school life and which encourage pupils to make a response.

Evaluating the effectiveness of the curriculum gives you useful information about how the school sees its role in preparing pupils for the next stage of their education as well as for their future adult life. An effective school uses all sources of information about its incoming pupils to make sure it tailors the curriculum to meet their needs. This is particularly important when children are coming to school for the first time.

The way the room is set out, particularly in the nursery, can give you a lot of information about the opportunities provided. For example, if the resources are clearly labelled and easily accessible to pupils, it is more likely that they will draw from them as needed in their work. There should be a good range of books, materials and equipment.

Find out how pupils with special educational needs are organised, for example in withdrawal groups, in classes with support, or in set groups, as the arrangements may make a difference to the curriculum pupils receive. Judge how well the curriculum is organised so as to meet the needs of pupils with SEN, taking particular note of the class teacher's provision, as this forms the basis for further interventions by the school or from outside the school. Check that the arrangements for using IEPs are effective in ensuring that individual needs are met while enabling pupils to have full access to the curriculum. There are likely to be specific arrangements to provide extra help for these pupils in literacy and numeracy and other communication skills, and for some of the pupils, help in gaining independence and mobility training, or extra help for those that are disturbed and need counselling. For pupils with statements, look at a representative sample by age and disability, and check that the provision in their statements is being implemented. In designated units or resource bases, judge whether the pupils' specific programmes are met, either by the class teacher in the base, or by the arrangements the school makes in all classes. Assess how well pupils in the unit are integrated in all aspects of the life of the school and whether the curricular arrangements promote inclusion of all pupils with SEN.

Does the school have effective strategies for teaching the basic skills of literacy and numeracy?

Every school is expected to have a strategy for teaching literacy and numeracy. Most schools reflect the National Literacy Strategy and the National Numeracy Strategy. Whether or not they do, you need to evaluate how effective their strategies are. In reaching this judgement you must take account of the results the school achieves in National Curriculum tests and any other assessments.

Does the school provide enrichment through its extra-curricular provision, including support for learning outside the school day?

The effective school will make arrangements to help all pupils take advantage of opportunities to learn, for example by visits out of school if used well, running after-school homework clubs and extra-curricular activities at different times of the day so that all pupils who wish to can attend. The range of extra-curricular opportunities often depends on the skills and availability of staff and parents, but usually encompasses, at least, some sort of sport and musical activity. The opportunity to take part and the number of pupils involved in all such activities will contribute to your evaluation.

Is the curriculum socially inclusive by ensuring equality of access and opportunity for all pupils?

You need to make sure that you have accurately defined the groups of pupils who form the intake of the school in THE CHARACTERISTICS OF THE SCHOOL. Once you have defined the groups, check if your preliminary analysis of performance and other output data indicate if there are any significant differences in the attainment, experience and benefit gained from what the school provides. If so use these to guide your observations, work sampling and discussions with pupils. Evaluate the extent to which:

- all pupils benefit according to need from what the school provides;

- any groups of pupils do not do as well as others and if the school is aware of this;

- the school offers justifiable explanations for any differences;

- the school has taken any effective action if needed.

☐ **For FULL INSPECTIONS only, the school's provision for personal, social and health education, and the quality of the school's links with the community and other schools, colleges and initial teacher training consortia**

Does the school provide for personal and social education, including health education, sex education and attention to drug misuse?

Schools must promote the spiritual, moral, social and cultural, mental and physical development of pupils at the school and prepare them for the opportunities, responsibilities and experience of adult life. This is achieved through the curriculum of the school, its ethos and its response to the individual needs of pupils.

You should establish whether provision is coherent, and appropriate to the ages and needs of pupils, and whether pupils have a sound knowledge and understanding of health issues, and an awareness of their ability to make choices relating to their health. Sex education may be an element of health education provision if the governors have decided to include it as part of the curriculum.

Schools are free to decide for themselves how best to organise drug education for their pupils. They may provide it within science lessons or, as appropriate, within other subject areas or as part of a broader programme of personal, social and health education. The essential aim of drug education should be to give pupils the facts, emphasise the benefits of a healthy lifestyle, and give them the knowledge and skills to make informed and healthy choices now and later in life.

Does the school have links with the community which contribute to pupils' learning?

Assess the different links the school has established and gauge if the school has done all it can to tap the resources available within its locality and beyond. Access to the Internet and well-developed skills in information and communications technology mean that many pupils now have enriching opportunities to link with others around the world. The school should be capitalising on these. Whenever possible, evaluate the school's involvement with the wider community, using such things as sporting or cultural events to broaden the experiences offered to pupils. There may be worthwhile visits out of school as well as inviting visitors and representatives of the community in to share their lifestyle and skills with pupils.

Does the school have constructive relationships with partner institutions such as link schools?

The most important link the school should have is with the children's families. Many primary and nursery schools, particularly those designated an Early Excellence Centre, will have other links, for example with visitors, playgroups, childminders, mother and toddler groups, and with other early years providers in the private and voluntary sectors. These links can be formal through a local Early Years Forum or informal and based on neighbourhood clusters which meet on a regular basis. Many primary schools have links with other local schools for all kinds of curriculum support, competitions, festivals and events which greatly enrich the curricular opportunities available to all pupils. Gauge the effectiveness of links with other schools the children have come from or to which they will transfer, particularly in relation to the transfer of their records and attainment data.

☐ How well the school cultivates pupils' personal – including spiritual, moral, social and cultural – development

Your evaluation of the provision for pupils' spiritual, moral, social and cultural development links these four aspects of personal development in which schools have an important part to play. Although each aspect of spiritual, moral, social and cultural development can be viewed separately, the provision is likely to be interconnected and your evaluation should reflect this. Your focus should be on what the school actively does to promote pupils' development in these aspects.

A good deal of your evidence for this section will come from your classroom observations. You need to be alert to situations which contribute to pupils' personal development and record them on your *Evidence Forms* so that you have a range of examples for possible inclusion in the written report.

Does the school provide pupils with knowledge and insights into values and beliefs, and enable them to reflect on their experiences in a way which develops their spiritual awareness and self-knowledge?

Assess how well the staff provide opportunities that help pupils explore the values of others. Young children will only be able to develop insight into the values and beliefs of others if their own ideas are valued by their peers, parents and teachers. As they get older, acceptance of these ideas continues in importance and spreads across all aspects of the curriculum, for example in stories, drama, art, music, history and religious education.

This is more likely to be developed well when pupils have opportunities to reflect on life's fundamental questions in ways appropriate to their age and stage of learning. Good teachers use events, such as the birth of a brother or sister or the death of a pet, to help pupils reflect on who we are, why we are here and our place in the world. You will need to judge how effectively the school plans to develop spiritual awareness. The pupils will usually be very keen to tell you about special moments in their lives. This does not need to have any religious connection, but in many schools, particularly church schools, religious education will make a significant contribution to pupils' spiritual development.

Collective worship

In all schools other than nursery schools, the law requires the provision of a daily act of collective worship. In denominational schools this will be inspected under section 23 School Inspections Act 1996. Evaluation should focus on whether the acts of worship are well planned and encourage pupils to explore questions about meaning and purpose, values and beliefs. Compliance with statutory requirements on collective worship will be recorded in *Form S3* by the school.

Taken over a term, the majority of such acts of worship should be wholly or mainly of a broadly Christian character. The school prospectus should make clear the parents' right to withdraw their children from collective worship. In forming a judgement about the character and quality of worship in schools, the following points may be helpful:

- worship is generally understood to imply the recognition of a supreme being. It should be clear that the words used and/or the activities observed in worship recognise the existence of a deity;

- collective worship should not be judged by the presence or absence of a particular ingredient. It might include: sharing values of a Christian nature; opportunities for prayers or meditation; opportunities to reflect upon readings from holy texts or other writings which bring out religious themes; and performance of music, drama and/or dance;

- each act of worship observed in the school should be considered together before reaching a judgement and then set alongside what is planned over a term. On balance, if it is judged that what the school provides is not in keeping with the spirit of the law, then this should be reported clearly;

- worship may be judged not to fulfil statutory requirements but could still be observed to make a powerful contribution to pupils' spiritual, moral, social and cultural development. If this is the case it should be explained in the report.

Does the school promote principles which distinguish right from wrong?

It is a fundamental responsibility of teachers and other adults who work with nursery and primary-age pupils to help them understand the difference between right and wrong. Moral development means that the child's actions are governed by an internalised set of principles and values rather than any fear of sanctions or craving for reward. With support, nursery children are aware of what is acceptable and unacceptable behaviour. Older pupils are able to make moral decisions through the application of reason, even though they may not cope quite so securely with problems in which they are emotionally involved. In other words, their learning about moral issues may be at a different point from their behaviour. Moral and social education are closely related and depend on the school promoting and fostering values such as honesty, fairness and respect for truth and justice.

Evaluate how effectively the school provides a moral code as a basis for behaviour which is promoted throughout the life of the school. Pupils should be given chances to develop and express moral values and extend their personal understanding across a range of issues, including equal opportunities and personal rights and responsibilities. Incidents which arise in school and well-chosen stories may also be useful in helping children distinguish between right and wrong behaviour.

Does the school encourage pupils to take responsibility, show initiative and develop an understanding of living in a community?

Schools which are effective in promoting the social development of their pupils provide many opportunities for them to take responsibility, show initiative and develop an understanding of living in a community. Whatever the age of the child, social competence hinges on the acceptance of group rules. Learning how to relate to others and to take responsibility for one's own actions is an important part of social education. The quality of the relationships in the school is of crucial importance in forming pupils' attitudes to good social behaviour and self-discipline.

Adults provide powerful role models for children and should, therefore, model the values such as courtesy and respect in all their dealings with other adults and pupils in the school. Assess how well the adults in the school encourage pupils to work together co-operatively, to compete fairly and to act on their own initiative. Look for the ways in which pupils are helped to take responsibility. In the nursery, this may include getting out and putting away resources or caring for living things such as plants or pets. For older pupils there may be chances to look after younger pupils or run activities such as fundraising for a charity. It may also include taking part as a member of a school council, with real opportunities to voice opinions and have them acted on.

Does the school teach the pupils to appreciate their own cultural traditions as well as the diversity and richness of other cultures?

The school's approach should be an active one. Look for evidence of how the school promotes the cultural traditions of its own area and the ethnic and cultural diversity of British society. You may see it in something as simple as teaching traditional playground games, or in capitalising on the skills of local artists, workers and residents of the area. Contributions to cultural development can come from all subjects of the curriculum as well as extra-curricular activities. Art, literature and music are often areas where traditions of other cultures can be drawn upon, appreciated and valued. These areas are enriched when the school is able to draw on people from different cultures and countries to share experiences with the pupils.

5. HOW WELL DOES THE SCHOOL CARE FOR ITS PUPILS?

Inspectors must evaluate and report on:

☐ the steps taken to ensure pupils' welfare, health and safety, including the school's arrangements for child protection;

☐ the effectiveness of the school's assessment and monitoring of pupils' academic performance, and monitoring of personal development and attendance;

☐ the effectiveness of the school's educational and personal support and guidance in raising pupils' achievements.

In determining their judgements, inspectors should consider the extent to which the school:

- ensures the health, safety, care and protection of all pupils;

- has effective measures to promote good attendance and behaviour, and to eliminate oppressive behaviour including all forms of harassment and bullying;

- has effective arrangements for assessing pupils' attainments and progress;

- uses its assessment information to guide its planning;

- provides effective support and advice for all its pupils, informed by the monitoring of their academic progress, personal development, behaviour and attendance;

- meets statutory requirements for day and residential provision where relevant or as outlined in a statement of special educational needs.

INSPECTION FOCUS

Focus your inspection on how effectively the school cares for its pupils, whatever their needs or circumstances, not just on the policies and systems. There are three components to the inspection of care and guidance:

■ the welfare and safety and child protection arrangements for pupils;

■ the assessment of pupils' academic and personal development, as well as their attendance;

■ the use of support and guidance to raise pupils' achievement.

Although much of the evidence you gather will be common to all three components, in SHORT INSPECTIONS you are only required to make judgements and report on the first of these, *unless* concerns emerge about the care of pupils. If you are concerned, you will need to explore these further.

In all inspections:

■ give priority to pupils' safety and protection, and in your report summary and commentary state any aspect of care which is a strength or weakness;

■ always report orally any shortcomings in health and safety matters to the governors. Do not publish any information that could jeopardise pupils' safety.

If pupils are not well cared for they will not be able to learn effectively. This is particularly true of the youngest children in nursery and primary schools who are much more dependent upon adults for their welfare. There are other particularly vulnerable pupils that the school needs to protect, for example those with special educational needs, those who are shy and withdrawn, and those who are known to be at risk.

From your pre-inspection analysis and initial visit you already know some of the challenges and issues the school faces. These will give a specific focus to your inspection.

MAKING JUDGEMENTS

In SHORT INSPECTIONS, take account of all the relevant criteria to come to your judgement about whether pupils' welfare is safeguarded, even though you are not required to report on them. This ensures that all aspects of welfare are considered.

The following characteristics illustrate where to pitch judgements about how well the school cares for its pupils.

Very good or better	Teachers know individual pupils very well, including those from particular groups or with SEN, and are fully aware of their physical, emotional and intellectual needs. They respond to them in a positive and supportive way. The day-to-day work of the school, in terms of supervision, awareness of hazards within and beyond the school, and the promotion of healthy living, creates a strong sense of the importance of health and safety of pupils. The school has effective practices to identify how well pupils are making progress, particularly in the core subjects, and the achievements of different groups. This identification is followed by good diagnosis of what such groups do well and how they might improve. The school has effective ways of being aware of developing patterns in pupils' behaviour or attendance and relating these patterns to achievement. The systematic monitoring of pupils leads to changes or modifications to the curriculum, for example, or to individual support for pupils' performance and development.
Satisfactory or better	Teachers know pupils well, recognise their needs and respond well to them. The working environment is safe and pupils are well supervised at work and at play. The school maintains records of pupils' achievements in most aspects of the core curriculum and individual action plans are in place and used for pupils with special education needs to monitor progress and guide teaching. The school promotes good behaviour and attendance through agreed, shared and successfully implemented policies. The monitoring the school carries out of pupils' performance and development is used to make changes in approach and emphasis.

The school's care of its pupils **cannot be satisfactory** if:

- it does not take reasonable steps to ensure the care of individual pupils and minimise the possibility of significant harm;

- it does not have satisfactory arrangements to track the progress of pupils in English and mathematics and take action to raise achievement;

- it does not adequately monitor and deal with problems of behaviour and attendance.

REPORTING REQUIREMENTS

SUMMARY REPORT	On all inspections you must complete the box, HOW WELL DOES THE SCHOOL CARE FOR ITS PUPILS?, in the table headed OTHER ASPECTS OF THE SCHOOL with comments on any particular strengths and weaknesses.
	If any of these are a feature of improvement in the school, record this in the section HOW THE SCHOOL HAS IMPROVED SINCE ITS LAST INSPECTION.
	Any aspects that are particularly good or need to improve should be reported under WHAT THE SCHOOL DOES WELL or WHAT COULD BE IMPROVED.
SHORT INSPECTIONS	Expand your judgements in the commentary as reported in either WHAT THE SCHOOL DOES WELL and WHAT COULD BE IMPROVED.
FULL INSPECTIONS	Report under the heading HOW WELL DOES THE SCHOOL CARE FOR ITS PUPILS?

On FULL INSPECTIONS, assessment and monitoring of pupils' academic performance and monitoring of personal development and attendance **must be considered unsatisfactory** if:

- the school is ineffective in assessing the pupils' attainments and does not track their progress in core subjects;

- the school is not effective in monitoring the pupils' personal development;

- the school does not adequately monitor and promote attendance, and does not take effective steps to reduce unauthorised absence.

Example 5.1

Extract from the inspection report on a full inspection of a first school

Teachers and support staff keep good records to keep track of the pupils' academic or personal development. They know the pupils well and have precise information to tell them what the pupils have done well or where they need help. As a consequence, support is directed effectively to the pupils who need it most. For example, the learning support assistant was directed to help the youngest reception pupils that needed assistance in getting undressed and dressed for physical education.

[Good assessment and support for pupils (3)]

On FULL INSPECTIONS, the effectiveness of the school's educational and personal support and guidance **must be considered unsatisfactory** if:

- the support and guidance to pupils fails to give attention to raising pupils' achievements and improving behaviour and attendance.

GUIDANCE ON USING THE CRITERIA

The following guidance provides further details for each of the criteria. Refer to these as appropriate to your inspection in the context of the particular school.

☐ **The steps taken to ensure pupils' welfare, health and safety, including the school's arrangements for child protection**

Does the school ensure the health, safety, care and protection of all pupils?

The quality of care is evident in *all* the relationships in the school, in teachers' knowledge of pupils and their needs, and how the school acts to promote the best interests of all its individual pupils. Take account of the four main principles which govern the Children Act and check whether they are understood by the school. These are that the school should:

- work in pupils' best interests to safeguard their welfare and promote their development;

- work in partnership with other responsible agencies to secure pupils' welfare;

- consider the wishes and feelings of those with parental responsibility;

- give due consideration to the child's religion, racial origin, cultural and linguistic background.

Pupils' welfare and safety are reflected in the quality of care they receive and the effectiveness of the school's arrangements to:

- ensure that each pupil is well known by at least one teacher, who links effectively with staff with key responsibilities in the school;

- ensure that all pupils and staff work in a safe environment;

- ensure child protection arrangements comply with procedures that are agreed locally;

- promote good attendance;

- promote good behaviour which is free from harassment and bullying;

- identify and meet individual needs, including those of pupils with special educational needs;

- promote healthy and safe living.

In all inspections, the data provided by the school will give you a starting point for your further investigations. For example, the data on attendance and exclusions and information from the headteacher's statement in *Form S4*, will give you important indicators.

When you walk around the school judge the safety of the environment for pupils and staff:

■ ask about the day-to-day working practices to ensure that pupils and staff are protected from harm;

■ check the health and safety policy is regularly monitored;

■ check the quality of supervision of young children during playtime, and before and after school, and the collection arrangements for young children.

Good schools will successfully build on their day-to-day arrangements in complying with procedures adopted by the local Area Child Protection Committee (ACPC). You should check whether:

■ staff are aware who the designated senior member of staff responsible is;

■ the school policy is in line with local procedures;

■ staff are aware of what to do if they suspect, or have disclosed to them, that an individual child may need protection;

■ the designated member of staff has detailed knowledge of local procedures;

■ staff know who the LEA responsible officer is;

■ staff have knowledge of the possible signs and symptoms of child abuse;

■ new staff are informed about what to do as part of their induction;

■ all staff receive in-service training to maintain and update their knowledge and understanding of procedures.

Find out how the school liaises with other agencies to monitor the progress of pupils on the 'at risk' register. For example, find out the arrangements for attending case conferences and for providing reports at the request of the ACPC on how individual children are getting on at school. In addition, you will find evidence in the school's curriculum to judge how the pupils are helped to look after themselves and to develop a responsible attitude as they grow up. If you find a school does not have effective procedures complying with those of the ACPC, explain any mis-match when it occurs. This must be reported to the headteacher and the governing body and included in the inspection report.

You will need to evaluate how successfully the school cares for pupils who are known to need particular attention and for whom the school needs to be especially vigilant. The school has a duty, for example, to ensure that the provision outlined in statements of SEN is implemented. The provision may require liaison with external SEN support staff and other agencies such as health authorities and social services departments. Other pupils with dietary or medical problems, or difficult home circumstances, may require the school to take particular care. Find out how well aware the school is of any pupils 'looked after' by the local authority, and how sensitively staff who need to know the particular circumstances liaise with carers.

In an effective school, staff will know in detail about the different needs of pupils and will provide consistent and convincing responses to your questions about what they do to help pupils, and how pupils are helped to look after themselves. Look at the impact the personal, social and health education programme has in helping pupils to be increasingly independent, self-confident and knowledgeable about themselves and healthy and safe living. If the school is part of the government's 'healthy school' initiative, you should be able to trace and evaluate the impact of this participation in the day-to-day work of the school. Look, for example, at how the school teaches pupils to remember their home address or telephone number in case they are lost, and how, in liaison with the police, they deal with strangers whom they may encounter.

Does the school have effective measures to promote good attendance and behaviour, and to eliminate oppressive behaviour such as all forms of harassment and bullying?

The priority that staff give to encouraging good attendance and behaviour is a strong indicator of the steps taken by the school to ensure pupils' welfare and safety. In nursery schools, see whether the staff work with parents and carers to ensure they bring and collect their children on time. In primary schools do class teachers encourage individual pupils to attend and be punctual, and is this backed up in assemblies, which are often occasions when the whole school is reminded about attendance? You may have picked up from the parents' questionnaire, or at the meeting before the inspection, how the school encourages parents to ensure their child's attendance.

In primary schools much of the responsibility for reminding pupils about how to behave well, and about their attitudes to others, rests with class teachers. Look at the evidence from HOW WELL ARE PUPILS TAUGHT? which tells you how successfully teachers minimise disruption and poor behaviour through their skilful handling of pupils in lessons and help pupils know what behaviour is expected of them. You should assess the impact of the school's statutory behaviour policy in promoting respect and tolerance towards others and their beliefs, cultures and ethnic backgrounds.

Check that the policy makes clear the school's intolerance of bullying and racial and sexual harassment. Check that policies for recording the pattern and frequency of racial incidents are in place and that such incidents and the actions taken are reported annually to the governing body, parents and the LEA. See how consistently staff reward pupils for good work and behaviour in and outside the school and, when there is poor behaviour, how consistently and appropriately sanctions are used in proportion to the misdemeanours.

Your observations around the school, in lessons, and in discussions with pupils will help you evaluate how the school eliminates oppressive behaviour, bullying and harassment. Ask for the records of any incidents that have taken place during the previous 12 months. Take particular note of the measures the school takes to prevent bullying, harassment and racial incidents. See whether, in your view, the measures are working. Check that no groups or individuals are unfairly treated and disadvantaged.

☐ **The effectiveness of the school's assessment and monitoring of pupils' academic performance, and monitoring of personal development and attendance**

Does the school have effective arrangements for assessing pupils' attainments and progress? Does it use its assessment information to guide its planning?

In FULL INSPECTIONS you should evaluate how effective the school is in assessing how well pupils are doing academically and how well they are developing in their personal skills.

For the younger pupils in nursery and reception classes, find out how they are assessed in relation to the Early Learning Goals and other aspects of their development, such as their disposition to learning. Usually this is done by regular observation and staff discussion involving all the nursery staff. The important issue is how well the assessments are used for planning. In reception classes, look at the outcomes of baseline assessment. See if teachers and other staff make assessment a natural part of the teaching and learning, and if the results are cross-checked regularly to ensure their validity. Find out how good teachers are at establishing a consensus about different levels of attainment in subjects in the National Curriculum, particular in English and mathematics. Check that assessment arrangements conform to what is required by QCA at 7 and 11 years of age.

Judge how well teachers assess pupils in all aspects of their work, behaviour and personal development and whether they have a full picture of their pupils' strengths and weaknesses. This should include qualities such as persistence, application, co-operation with others, ability to concentrate, and self-confidence. Check how well subject and assessment co-ordinators work together with class teachers so that consistent records are produced and made use of throughout the school to guide planning.

See how effectively the school builds on its assessment procedures when identifying pupils with SEN to comply with the Code of Practice. Judge how effective and consistent the procedures are for placing pupils on the register, and for deciding what further help is needed in accordance with the school's SEN policy and the guidance in the Code.

Judge how well the school monitors the results of its assessments so as to identify the achievements of different ethnic groups by ability or by gender. Check how well this information is recorded and analysed (particularly in providing support for EAL) to help the school take action to improve achievement. If there is no evidence of monitoring the achievement of different groups of pupils, it raises questions about how effective the school is in meeting the needs of all the pupils.

Look at how the school monitors its attendance and analyses the attendance data. Do teachers understand what constitutes authorised absence? How consistent are they in recording unauthorised absence?

If exclusions take place, is the governing body properly involved, and what action does the school take to review its practice, if necessary? Parents should be kept informed about the behaviour policy at least annually.

☐ The effectiveness of a school's educational and personal support and guidance in raising pupils' achievements

Does the school provide effective support and advice for all its pupils, informed by the monitoring of their academic progress, personal development, behaviour and attendance?

In FULL INSPECTIONS, your judgement on how effectively the school supports pupils to raise their achievements relies on what you have already found out about assessment practice and the use made of assessment. What does the school do to acknowledge pupils' achievements, particularly when great strides in progress have taken place? Evaluate the effect this has on encouraging pupils to achieve more.

Find out and assess how well the school identifies what action it can take to help individuals or groups of pupils, for example through changes to the day-to-day organisation and through the provision of extra help. Does the school discuss what it knows about pupils' strengths and weaknesses with the pupils themselves, and with parents and other agencies? In primary schools, much emphasis will be placed on how well pupils achieve in literacy and numeracy. Assess how carefully the school deals with pupils who need to improve their skills in literacy and numeracy and how, in liaison with parents, they are encouraged, yet challenged, to improve. If targets are set for individual pupils, do they focus only on attainment or also on other specific aspects of their life at school, such as their behaviour or attendance? Check that the targets are clear and can be monitored for success. Make sure the school discriminates between those occasions where outside agencies must be asked for help (for example, child protection) and where it is reasonable for the school to provide support internally.

Does the school meet the statutory requirements for day and residential provision where relevant or as outlined in a statement of special educational needs?

Your pre-inspection work on the characteristics of the school should alert you to those pupils who have statements of SEN. Evidence from the section on HOW GOOD ARE THE CURRICULAR AND OTHER OPPORTUNITIES OFFERED TO PUPILS? should help you in making this judgement. You should make sure that you scrutinise pupils' statements; all of them when there are five or less, and no less than half when numbers are greater, so that a representative sample by age and disability is looked at. You should check that the statements or reviews are up to date so that you know that the provision outlined in the statement is implemented by the school and any other agency involved, such as speech therapists or LEA support staff. Any evident shortfall in the provision should be further checked to find out why this is so. Ensure that specific disability-related provision is implemented, such as aids for hearing, seeing, writing or to facilitate mobility or for specific arrangements in respect of personal hygiene. Check that access to additional staffing indicated in the statement is available and used effectively. Make sure that specific curricular arrangements are met such as work in literacy, numeracy and oracy and that, overall, pupils have their entitlement to a broad and balanced curriculum. Check that arrangements specified in the statement for ensuring that pupils have full access to the whole of the school's curriculum are in place. Where residential provision is specified, check that the arrangements provided by the school match the statement, particularly in respect of the number of nights boarding, regularity of contact with pupils' parents or carers, and specified programmes, for example to boost independence or self-care skills. You need to be sure that suitable arrangements ensure that all key members of staff who need to know the provision are aware of the contents of the statement and are able subsequently to contribute to any review that takes place. If it is possible to attend an annual or transition review during the inspection it will demonstrate if the provision is re-examined in the light of any progress made and that key people attend as appropriate.

6. HOW WELL DOES THE SCHOOL WORK IN PARTNERSHIP WITH PARENTS?

Inspectors must evaluate and report on:

☐ parents' and carers' views of the school;

☐ the effectiveness of the school's links with parents and carers;

☐ the impact of the parents' and carers' involvement with the work of the school.

In determining their judgements, inspectors should consider the extent to which:

- parents and carers are satisfied with what the school provides and achieves;

- parents and carers are provided with good quality information about the school, and particularly about pupils' progress;

- links with parents and carers, including the use of home–school agreements, contribute to pupils' learning at school and at home.

INSPECTION FOCUS

Parents depend on the school to provide well for their children. You need to find out whether they feel the school lives up to their expectations and responds to any concerns.

Where a school uses the OFSTED parents' questionnaire you will be able to evaluate how parents feel about the main aspects of the school. You need to use your professional judgement as to the number of responses to a question that signify an important strength or weakness as perceived by parents. The responses to the questionnaire will indicate where you may need more information and issues you may want to follow up at the parents' meeting.

The best opportunity for parents to share their views with you comes at the meeting for parents who have children at the school. Use this meeting:

- to explore the views of parents on those aspects of the school specified in the inspection schedule;

- to follow up issues from the parents' responses to the questionnaire;

- to allow parents to tell you what they think about the school;

- to judge whether there are groups of parents who have not been heard and to provide an opportunity for their views to be heard.

There are many other opportunities for you to find out what parents think of the school. For instance:

- parents may request to see you or speak to you on the telephone during an inspection;

- talking with parents who work and help in the school;

- talking with parents at the beginning and the end of the school day when they bring and collect their children;

- by visiting events held for parents by the school during the period of the inspection.

On SHORT INSPECTIONS, you are only required to follow up the areas relating to issues raised by parents' views that seem from the parents' meeting and questionnaire to be important.

On FULL INSPECTIONS, evaluate also: how well the school involves parents and carers as partners in their children's learning; and the quality and effectiveness of the information it provides for parents and carers, and particularly the effect these have on improving pupils' achievements, including their personal development.

Evaluate how well the school consults parents and carers about its curriculum provision and about major spending decisions. This will tell you about the application of the principle of consultation within the best value framework.

MAKING JUDGEMENTS

To make your judgements, use all the evidence you have about the parents' level of satisfaction with the school, the effectiveness of the school's partnership with them and the contribution that this partnership makes to pupils' learning.

Consider this alongside the other evidence and judgements that you have made in HOW WELL DOES THE SCHOOL CARE FOR ITS PUPILS? In particular, examine those judgements you have made on the effectiveness of support and advice provided by the school for its pupils and how well parents are able to use this information to help their children learn.

The following characteristics illustrate where to pitch judgements about how well the school works in partnership with parents and carers.

Very good or excellent	The school has a very good range of productive and consistent links with parents and carers that help pupils learn. These extend from involvement in hearing individual children read to, for example, homework projects and workshops. The mechanisms for exchanging information between school and home work very well and include opportunities for parents and carers to give information to the school about their child. Information to parents and carers through written reports is excellent, making clear what pupils need to do to improve and how parents can help. There is strong parental satisfaction with the school, based on secure understanding and regular involvement in its work. There is evidence of improvement in children's learning, behaviour and personal development resulting from good liaison with parents and carers.
Satisfactory or better	The school has effective links with parents and carers to consolidate and extend pupils' learning. Parents are, in the main, satisfied with the standards achieved and what the school provides, with no major concerns. Reports to parents are clear and useful, and the exchange of information is sound.

However, the partnership with parents **cannot be satisfactory** if:

- there is a significant degree of dissatisfaction among parents about the school's work, which is supported by inspection findings;

- information to parents and carers does not give a clear view of children's progress, particularly in English and mathematics;

- parents are kept at arm's length and the school makes little effort to communicate with them and involve them in the life of the school.

Example 6.1

Extract from Record of Corporate Judgements *on a short inspection of a primary school*

Strengths:

- *Large number of parents help in school, well-targeted to meet needs of all pupils, particularly in reading*

- *Parents like way school values all pupils whatever their ability; extra-curricular activities; community spirit.*

Sources of evidence:

- *Parents' meeting; parents' questionnaire; EFs on discussion with parent helpers and HT*

- *Parents' meeting and parents' questionnaire*

Weaknesses:

- *Homework policy not clear*

- *Information about the curriculum*

Sources of evidence:

- *Parents' questionnaire*

- *Parents' meeting*

Overall evaluation:

Parents support the school in many ways and value what it provides for their children. Inspection supports parents' views about homework and curriculum information.

[Good links with parents (3)]

Example 6.2

Extract from a full inspection report on a middle school

Parents are kept well informed about school events through a regular newsletter. There are too few opportunities for parents to make informal contacts with the school other than at the school gate at the beginning and end of the school day. This largely superficial contact with parents means that they do not feel encouraged to participate in school. There are no helpers in classrooms and considerable difficulty in persuading parents to stand as governors. Parents, therefore, have little impact on the school.

[Poor involvement and links with parents (6)]

REPORTING REQUIREMENTS

SUMMARY REPORT	All inspectors must complete the table headed PARENTS' VIEW OF THE SCHOOL, and state the extent to which the inspection team agrees with parents' views. If the school's work with parents and carers is a feature of improvement in the school, record this in the section HOW THE SCHOOL HAS IMPROVED SINCE ITS LAST INSPECTION.
	Any aspect that is particularly good or needs to improve should be reported under WHAT THE SCHOOL DOES WELL and WHAT COULD BE IMPROVED.
SHORT INSPECTIONS	Only parents' and carers' views of the school are reported. Expand any points made in the commentary under WHAT THE SCHOOL DOES WELL and WHAT COULD BE IMPROVED.
FULL INSPECTIONS	Report under the heading HOW WELL DOES THE SCHOOL WORK IN PARTNERSHIP WITH PARENTS?

GUIDANCE ON USING THE CRITERIA

☐ Parents' views of the school

Are parents satisfied with what the school provides and achieves?

You need to establish how far parents are satisfied with the quality and effectiveness of what the school provides and achieves. Decide whether the inspection evidence supports or refutes the views of parents and why. These judgements must then be reported in the summary and, as appropriate, in Part B of the report.

On SHORT INSPECTIONS, you are unlikely to have much time for more detailed work on the quality of the partnership between parents and the school. Where you do find evidence, for instance when examining information provided by the school for parents, you may want to take it into account. On SHORT INSPECTIONS, you should only follow up those areas of the school's relationship with parents that seem from the meeting and questionnaire to be burning issues or that shed important light on what the school does well or not so well.

☐ The effectiveness of the school's links with parents

☐ The impact of parents' involvement with the work of the school

Are parents provided with good-quality information about the school, and particularly about pupils' progress?

On a FULL INSPECTION, you must evaluate the effectiveness and impact of the school's partnership with parents. The good school sees parents as a rich resource with an important contribution to make and helps them to support their children's learning. The way in which the school does this, and the extent to which the school and parents work together, will have an effect on how well pupils make progress in school.

You must evaluate the extent to which the school actively draws in all parents. This includes those from minority ethnic backgrounds, especially those who do not speak English as a first language, and encourages them to support their children's learning. Your starting point and the source of issues you wish to pursue will be the parents' responses to the questionnaire and their contributions to the parents' meeting. Further evidence will emerge from:

- talking with parents before and after school;

- meeting with parents who work and help in the school and on school visits and finding out how the school 'trains' and prepares parents who are involved;

- talking with parent governors and any representatives from parents' associations and clubs;

- how far information provided for parents can be understood and used;

- how well the school keeps in touch with parents who speak little English.

Do links with parents, including the use of home–school agreements, contribute to pupils' learning at school and at home?

An effective partnership includes the sharing of information about children, their learning and how they feel about school. If any visits are made to children and parents before children enter school, evaluate the impact of these on both the parents and children. Find out whether the induction programmes, particularly in nursery and reception, are flexible enough to suit the needs of all children. Evaluate the extent to which parents with toddlers and babies are encouraged to come into school, and how easy it is for parents to borrow books and other resources for children. Examine the effectiveness of arrangements for contacts with pupils' homes, to identify and help children who are unhappy, and for involving parents who rarely come near the school.

Assessing the quality of information provided for parents is one part of this evaluation. Examine, for instance:

■ any policies on home–school contracts and the extent to which they work;

■ what account the school takes of what parents know about their own child's learning;

■ how far parents and teachers can talk informally together about children, and the arrangements that are made for parents whose first language is not English;

■ whether reports to parents about pupils' progress tell them clearly what their children are doing, how well they are doing it, whether it is good enough and what they need to do to improve;

■ to what extent written reports are followed up and discussed with parents;

■ the extent to which pupils' reports and records incorporate the views of parents and show the action agreed to help pupils learn;

■ how well the school helps parents to understand what is taught;

■ the extent to which any home–school agreements contribute to pupils' learning;

■ the extent to which parents know about and use lending libraries for toys and books;

■ whether parents of children with special educational needs are properly involved in identifying their needs, provide appropriate support and regularly review their child's progress;

■ how well the school communicates with parents who have disabilities, learning difficulties or who live a long way from the school without easy transport;

■ how well the school consults parents about its curriculum and about major spending decisions within its application of the consultation principle in the best value framework.

7. HOW WELL IS THE SCHOOL LED AND MANAGED?

Inspectors must evaluate and report on:

- ☐ how efficiently and effectively the headteacher and key staff lead and manage the school, promoting high standards and effective teaching and learning;

- ☐ how well the governing body fulfils its statutory responsibilities and accounts for the performance and improvement of the school;

- ☐ how effectively the school monitors and evaluates its performance, diagnoses its strengths and weaknesses and takes effective action to secure improvements;

- ☐ the extent to which the school makes the best strategic use of its resources, including specific grants and additional funding, linking decisions on spending to educational priorities;

- ☐ the extent to which the principles of best value are applied in the school's use of resources;

- ☐ the adequacy of staffing, accommodation and learning resources, highlighting strengths and weaknesses in different subjects and areas of the curriculum where they affect the quality of education provided and the educational standards achieved.

In determining their judgements, inspectors should consider the extent to which:

- leadership ensures clear direction for the work and development of the school, and promotes high standards;

- the school has explicit aims and values, including a commitment to good relationships and equality of opportunity for all, which are reflected in all its work;

- there is rigorous monitoring, evaluation and development of teaching;

- there is effective appraisal and performance management;

- the school identifies appropriate priorities and targets, takes the necessary action, and reviews progress towards them;

- there is a shared commitment to improvement and the capacity to succeed;

- governors fulfil their statutory duties in helping to shape the direction of the school and have a good understanding of its strengths and weaknesses;

- educational priorities are supported through careful financial management;

- good delegation ensures the effective contribution of staff with management responsibilities;

- effective use is made of new technology, including information and communications technology (ICT);

- specific grant is used effectively for its designated purpose(s);

- the number, qualifications and experience of teachers and support staff match the demands of the curriculum;

- the accommodation allows the curriculum to be taught effectively;

- learning resources are adequate for the school's curriculum and range of pupils;

- there is effective induction of staff new to the school and the school is, or has the potential to be, an effective provider of initial teacher training;

- the best value principles of comparison, challenge, consultation and competition are applied in the school's management and use of resources.

INSPECTION FOCUS

Good schools are led and managed for the benefit of all their pupils. Your inspection must focus on the extent to which leadership and management create an effective and improving school where pupils are keen and able to learn. You must evaluate impact rather than intention and ensure that your judgements on the effectiveness of leadership and the efficiency of management make sense when set against your judgements about standards, teaching and learning, and other aspects of the school covered elsewhere in the *Evaluation Schedule*.

In all inspections focus on:

- the effectiveness of leadership and the efficiency of management as distinctive elements, provided by the headteacher, staff with management responsibilities and governors;

- the effect of leadership and management on the quality and standards of education;

- how well the school understands its strengths and weaknesses through its own monitoring and evaluation;

- the school's commitment to improvement;

- the appraisal and performance management of the headteacher and other staff.

In SHORT INSPECTIONS, where the school is usually very effective, evaluate why it is, and find out what the leaders and managers do that works.

Note: The guidance on the aspects of management, particularly performance management, will be amended as further details become available about the implementation of the 1998 Green Paper.

MAKING JUDGEMENTS

Your overall judgements about how well the school is led and managed should take account of *Form S4* and must tie in with what else you have found out about the school. There is usually, but not always, a clear relationship between the standards achieved and the effectiveness of those who lead and manage. Evaluate the extent to which this causality applies.

The following characteristics illustrate where to pitch judgements about how well the school is led and managed.

Very good or excellent	The leader(s) of the school share a common purpose and put pupils and their achievements first. They build co-operative and co-ordinated teams and use assessment evidence well to set high goals for pupils and challenging targets for the school and for individual staff. Staff in the school reflect critically on what they can do to improve learning and develop more effective ways of working. The work of the school is fully and thoroughly monitored, particularly the quality of teaching and its impact, and the behaviour of pupils. There is good delegation to staff with management responsibilities and effective follow-up to ensure tasks are completed well. Governors monitor performance and have a good understanding of the strengths and weaknesses of the school and the challenges it faces, and set the right priorities for development and improvement. They fulfil their statutory duties well in providing a sense of direction for the school. They understand and apply best value principles.
Satisfactory or better	The leadership and management of the school are clear about its strengths and weaknesses and have established some ways of securing improvement in the average level of standards achieved. Teamwork is well established in the main and the school has identified the right tasks for the future. Most staff share a common purpose and have taken steps to make their work more effective. Staff with particular responsibilities are clear about what these are and how they will measure their success. Governors have a sound sense of the strengths and weaknesses of the school and are working with staff in their efforts to improve. They meet their statutory responsibilities.

However, the leadership and management are **unlikely to be satisfactory** if any of these are present:

- there is a significant amount of unsatisfactory teaching;

- there is significant complacency among staff;

- standards in the school are significantly lower than they should be;

- the headteacher, senior managers and governors do not know the strengths and weaknesses of the school fairly accurately and therefore are largely ineffective.

Example 7.1

Extract from a short inspection report on a middle school

One of the main reasons for the recent successes of the school is the outstanding leadership provided by its senior managers and governors, and especially by the headteacher. The headteacher brings a very clear vision of what sort of school this should be. This ensures that pupils achieve their best and try to do better. Staff and pupils are committed to learning and have high expectations of success. Everything the school does seeks high quality. This vision is shared by governors, the deputy headteacher and other senior managers. The upward trend in the standards achieved by its pupils is just one way in which the school has been successful in fulfilling its aims.

[Excellent leadership and management (1)]

REPORTING REQUIREMENTS

SUMMARY REPORT	In both FULL and SHORT INSPECTIONS complete the table HOW WELL IS THE SCHOOL LED AND MANAGED?
	Comment on the strengths and weaknesses in leadership and management and evaluate briefly the extent to which the school applies the principles of best value.
	If any of these are features of improvement in the school report this in the section HOW THE SCHOOL HAS IMPROVED SINCE ITS LAST INSPECTION.
	If any aspects of leadership or management are particularly good or need to improve you must report these under WHAT THE SCHOOL DOES WELL or WHAT COULD BE IMPROVED.
	In FULL INSPECTIONS you must include a summary judgement about the adequacy of staffing, accommodation and learning resources.
SHORT INSPECTIONS	In the commentary expand your judgements on leadership and management as reported in either WHAT THE SCHOOL DOES WELL or WHAT COULD BE IMPROVED.
FULL INSPECTIONS	Report comprehensively under the heading HOW WELL IS THE SCHOOL LED AND MANAGED?

When reporting on leadership and management in a FULL INSPECTION, your evaluation must reflect all the criteria. The challenge for inspectors is to give a cohesive account rather than rehearsing findings in terms of each criterion, item by item.

Example 7.2

> ### Extract from a full inspection report on a primary school
>
> *The results of the National Curriculum tests have fluctuated over the last three years. The headteacher, governors and staff link this to the different abilities of year groups and have not analysed performance data to confirm their view. Co-ordinators order resources and ensure that materials are readily available to support learning in their subjects but they do not play any part in the monitoring of standards. As a consequence, the reasons for variations in standards are not known by the school and it sees no reason to take action to identify or remedy any weaknesses in its provision. Initiatives are followed without any clear idea of the benefits they may bring. For example, the literacy hour is now taught in every class and the headteacher and governors anticipate that this, in itself, will raise standards. They have not, however, monitored the introduction of this strategy and are not aware that teachers with poor phonological knowledge avoid teaching word-level work. This slows the pupils' progress and limits the strategies available to them when they learn to read and to spell unfamiliar words making the impact of the strategy on standards barely perceptible. The needs of the pupils are not paramount and little has been done to ensure that the education provided enables them to attain high standards.*
>
> [Poor monitoring and evaluation (7)]

GUIDANCE ON USING THE CRITERIA

In all inspections the first evidence for your evaluation comes from your earliest contacts with the school. Use the school's documentation, *Forms S3* and *S4*, the previous inspection report and the *PICSI report* information to formulate some of the initial questions and hypotheses about the work and development of the school and the extent to which it promotes high standards and effective teaching and learning.

☐ **How efficiently and effectively the headteacher and key staff lead and manage the school, promoting high standards and effective teaching and learning**

Leadership is concerned with:

■ creating and securing commitment to a clear vision;

■ managing change so as to improve the school;

■ building a high-performing team;

■ inspiring, motivating and influencing staff;

■ leading by example and taking responsibility.

Management is concerned with:

- strategic thinking and planning;

- people, including performance management; making best use of the skills of staff; delegation, appraisal and development;

- financial and other resources;

- communication;

- monitoring and evaluating performance and delivering results.

You need to distinguish between leadership and management when considering the operation of the school, although the two overlap.

Do leadership and management ensure a clear direction for the work and development of the school and promote high standards?

You need to establish what is the headteacher's vision for the school and how far the headteacher and senior staff give a firm steer to the school's work. Apply the same perspective to the work of other co-ordinators and evaluate the extent to which the headteacher's leadership helps them to do a good job. Development and improvement planning should reflect the school's stated aims and objectives and promote high standards.

Example 7.3

Extract from the registered inspector's Notebook _for the inspection of a large primary school_

• HT has poor relationship with governing body focusing on keeping finances in order [W]	EFs recording discussion with governors and HT
• HT's presence around the school ensures smooth running from day to day [S]	EF Nos JS3, JS8, JS11
• HT's management of staff sensitive and promotes professional development [S]	EFs recording discussion with staff
• DH takes lead on curriculum with HT passive [W]	EFs recording discussions with HT role and DH
• School's development plan focuses only on next year with little after that [W]	SDP

[Satisfactory management (4) but poor leadership (6)]

The evaluations that you have undertaken so far will enable you to begin to judge what aspects of standards and the success of pupils can be traced back to the impact of the school's leaders and managers. Where there are weaknesses in the work of the school and particularly what you see in classes, you should track these issues back to see how well the weaknesses are understood by senior staff and what they have done about them.

Does the school have explicit aims and values, including a commitment to good relationships and equality of opportunity for all, which are reflected in all its work?

You will see a great deal in your first contact with the school which brings to life the aims stated in its prospectus. Evidence will come from: how the headteacher, teaching and non-teaching staff and pupils interact with each other; signs of staff and pupils being valued and the school's commitment to inclusive policies; the welcome given to visitors; the quality and care of the school environment; and pride shown in the school by staff and pupils.

In lessons, look for a sense of purpose and signs that what the school and its management stand for are reflected in teaching, for example in the approaches taken to meet the needs of different individual pupils and groups.

Talk to staff and pupils about their views of the school and what it stands for, equal opportunities, and the extent to which senior staff are interested in their work.

Is there a shared commitment to improvement and capacity to succeed?

In order to establish the school's commitment to improvement and its capacity to succeed, assess:

■ whether or not standards and the expectations of teachers are high enough;

■ the headteacher's skills of leadership, decision-making and communication;

■ how far the headteacher and senior staff in the school know what needs to be done to improve, in what order of priority and how to do it;

■ how aware the staff are of what needs to be done, and how they can improve;

■ whether there is a determination by the staff to raise standards.

Does good delegation ensure the effective contribution of staff with management responsibilities?

If there are strengths or weaknesses in the work of staff responsible for co-ordination and development, explain what these are. In smaller schools the responsibilities sometimes are carried informally and staff often hold more than one. Consider the extent to which good delegation ensures the staff with management responsibilities contribute effectively. A good headteacher ensures that these responsibilities are clearly stated, often in job descriptions, and are effectively carried out. Look for evidence that delegation of work carries specific responsibilities and defined outcomes suited to the needs of the school, and is properly resourced.

In a very effective school, staff, including support staff, know their role in its day-to-day work and longer-term improvement.

Example 7.4

> **Extract from a short inspection report on a junior school**
>
> *All staff with management responsibilities work together well as a team. They all have clear written descriptions of what is expected of them and these are reviewed annually. The management team meets regularly and deals with long-term strategy. The headteacher allocates time for them to carry out their management roles and expects high-quality creative input in return. The deputy head and co-ordinators use considerable initiative in bringing new ideas to their work. They do not share these with the rest of the staff early enough and this reduces their impact on improving classroom practice.*
>
> [Good delegation and contribution of staff with responsibilities (3)]

One indication of the headteacher's competence and confidence is the way the run up to the inspection has been managed. Has the headteacher taken it in his or her stride, not allowing it to be too much of a distraction to staff and to the school's work and purpose, or has the inspection prompted unnecessary work and been allowed to induce unnecessary stress? Is the on-site inspection managed well by the school?

☐ **How well the governing body fulfils its statutory responsibilities and is able to account for the performance of the school**

How well do the governors fulfil their statutory duties in helping to shape the direction of the school and do they have a good understanding of its strengths and weaknesses?

The governing body has specific statutory responsibilities and its main tasks are: to provide a sense of direction for the work of the school; to support the work of the school as a critical friend; and to hold the school to account for the standards and quality of education it achieves.

The way in which the role of the governing body, or other appropriate authority, is interpreted may vary significantly in relation to the school size and type, and such factors as the experience of the chair of governors and other governors. Definitions of the role of the governing body are set out in education law; the issue for you is how effectively these roles are interpreted in the context of the particular school. For example, some nursery schools have an advisory committee whose roles and responsibilities will differ from those of a statutory governing body. If this is the case find out what kind of body it is and where its responsibilities lie.

In all inspections, your evaluation of the work of the governing body will need to take account of:

■ the context of the school and any impact this may have on the balance of skills, competence and commitment found in the work of governors;

■ the way the governing body ensures that the school meets statutory requirements;

■ the relationship between the work of the headteacher and senior managers and that of the governing body;

■ the extent to which the governing body appraises the work of the headteacher and sets performance targets for him or her.

Your evidence will come from your discussions with the chair and other members of the governing body (including teacher governors), the headteacher and staff about:

■ the way they exercise their corporate role;

■ how well they fulfil their statutory duties;

■ how they help to shape the direction of the school;

■ their knowledge of the strengths and weaknesses of the school and understanding of the challenges it faces;

■ whether appropriate priorities for development and improvement are set;

■ how well they have responded to the previous inspection;

■ how governors find out for themselves how things are going;

■ whether or not they take responsibility for good and poor aspects of the school.

Example 7.5

Extract from a short inspection report on a primary school

The governors contribute substantially to the effectiveness of the school. They have high levels of expertise and are very well organised and thorough in their approach. They are also open to new ideas and adapt quickly. This enables them to seize opportunities when they arise, such as bidding for 'seed money' for projects. They have trust in the headteacher but expect him to be fully accountable to them. They, in turn, account well to the parents of the school. The governors are active and keep themselves very well informed about what is going on in the school. They make regular visits and report back to meetings of the governing body.

[Overall: a very effective governing body (1)]

☐ **How effectively the school monitors and evaluates its performance, diagnoses its strengths and weaknesses, and takes effective action to secure improvement**

Is there rigorous monitoring, evaluation and development of teaching?

In all inspections you must assess how far and why the school's evaluation of teaching leads to development and improvement. Your starting points will come from *Form S4*, the last report and your judgements of standards and teaching. Look for improvement in teaching in what were the weakest subjects at the time of the last inspection and see if standards are rising. Consider:

■ the extent to which teachers are helped to analyse and draw on the approaches that work best with particular pupils;

■ how far the school knows and uses the strengths of its best teachers to influence the rest;

■ the ways in which the headteacher and other senior staff are involved, and know what is happening, in classrooms;

- whether appraisal of teachers, including newly qualified teachers (NQTs), contributes to the monitoring of teaching;

- the extent to which the headteacher's view of good and weak teaching is reflected in the work of the school;

- how well the school helps teachers and support staff to work together;

- whether performance targets are set for teachers.

Your evaluation must answer the following questions:

- How well does the school monitor and analyse its standards?

- What does it do with the information?

- How well does it evaluate the quality of teaching?

- Does it face up to its weaknesses and take adequate steps to overcome them?

- What impact does all this have?

Example 7.6

Extract from a full inspection report on a primary school

The headteacher's monitoring of teaching is too general to reveal the undemanding level of much of the work in mathematics, and doesn't probe how effectively mental arithmetic is taught. Monitoring is not specific enough to evaluate pupils' progress in numeracy and to identify where teaching needs to be accelerated. It has done little to improve the percentage of pupils attaining Level 2 in the National Curriculum tests.

[Overall: poor monitoring of teaching (6)]

Is there effective induction of staff new to the school and is the school, or has it the potential to be, an effective provider of initial teacher training?

From September 1999 all newly qualified teachers (NQTs) must have a 90 per cent teaching load, an induction tutor and identified written targets from regular observations.

A school could be an effective provider of initial teacher training when:

- it has professional development systems in place that are a good influence on standards of teaching;

- it is judged to be effective overall and to have improved since its previous inspection;

- it has a shared commitment to improvement and the capacity to succeed.

Is there effective appraisal and performance management?

The governing body is responsible for ensuring that the headteacher is appraised and targets are set, and that the school implements national requirements for the appraisal and pay of teachers. Where you have identified important weaknesses in the performance of teachers these systems are clearly not as effective as they need to be. Evidence of effective systems for managing teachers' performance will be seen when:

■ the deployment of resources rewards and motivates good teachers;

■ teachers work in harmony towards common goals;

■ management problems are tackled squarely;

■ capability/competency procedures are used to deal with poor performance;

■ strategies are in place to reduce staff absence;

■ appraisal and regular review assess performance through classroom observation.

From September 1999 governing bodies have been required to operate an appraisal system for headteachers and to set targets which arise from that appraisal. You will need to evaluate their arrangements for effective appraisal.

Does the school identify appropriate priorities and targets, take the necessary action and review progress towards them?

Effective headteachers identify the right development priorities based on a clear analysis of strengths and weaknesses. In all schools you need to evaluate how far the staff know the right things to do to improve performance and whether or not they do them.

Governing bodies have to set targets for their school, that is establish specific measurable goals for improved performance by pupils. These need to be agreed with the LEA. You must evaluate how well the school uses assessment and performance data to predict potential, focus effort and support improvement. Schools vary greatly in character and each finds its own particular way to raise achievement. This process is likely to be the most effective if it involves all staff. Where a school knows how good its standards are and how good its teaching is, it is well placed to set targets for itself, take the necessary action and review progress towards them.

Much of your evidence for the effectiveness of target setting will derive from your evaluation of how high standards are and whether they are high enough. Examine in particular the extent to which:

■ the school makes good use of entry profiles and baseline assessment;

■ information from standardised tests is used effectively;

■ the school questions itself about the performance of different individuals and groups of pupils, and reviews its own performance against that for other schools, and present as against past performance;

■ the school's priorities and targets are appropriate and linked with clear programmes of action;

■ procedures are in place to monitor the outcomes of this work.

☐ **The extent to which the school makes best strategic use of its resources, including specific grants and additional funding, linking decisions on spending to educational priorities**

How well are educational priorities supported through careful financial planning?

An efficient school demonstrates that it budgets systematically for all expenditure and is clear about the cost of its development. Your emphasis should not be on the detail of the financial planning, but rather on the extent to which the school's spending decisions relate to priorities for improvement and benefit for pupils. Once priorities have been identified you will need to find out the extent to which the school has applied the best value principle of competition in, for example, obtaining tenders for services or goods (*see Annex 1*).

Your overriding judgement on the use the school makes of its financial resources and newly developed technologies will be on how far all pupils benefit from wisely targeted spending. Much of the evidence you require for this judgement will be found in lessons.

If you need to investigate further, detailed school information will be found in *Form S2* and must be supplemented by discussion with appropriate staff in the school, particularly the finance officer, where this is not the headteacher. Your evaluation will concentrate on the logic and quality of links between planning and spending.

Another feature of careful financial planning is effective financial control and administration. You are not conducting a detailed financial audit but you must have access to the latest auditors' report. Establish whether:

■ the main recommendations in the report have been acted upon;

■ systems for financial administration are unobtrusive, efficient and responsive to need;

■ financial administration keeps the way clear for teachers to concentrate on their work;

■ adequate information is available to the headteacher and governors to ensure that finances are kept in good order and costs easily determined.

Example 7.7

Extract from a **Record of Corporate Judgements** *in the short inspection of an infant school*

Strengths:

- Recent audit report found efficient financial management and no significant weaknesses

- Resource allocations and educational priorities agreed together at the same time

- Development plan clearly listed and regularly updated

- HT and SMT evaluate spending in relation to improvement in standards

Weaknesses:

- GB relies too heavily on HT and is not very active in evaluating its spending

Sources of evidence:

- Audit

- Governors' minutes

- SDP; EF recording discussion with chair of finance

- EFs recording discussion with SMT

Sources of evidence:

- EF recording discussion with HT and GB

[Overall: good use of financial planning and resources (3)]

Is effective use made of new technologies, including ICT?

During the inspection ask about the use the school is making of new technologies, including ICT, electronic mail, multimedia compositions, data analysis, CD-ROM, the National Grid for Learning, and Internet applications. Evaluate the role of senior staff in ensuring the effective use of this technology.

Are specific grants used effectively for their designated purpose?

Where a school is in receipt of a specific grant, for instance the Ethnic Minorities Achievement Grant (EMAG), evaluate how well the school is using this money for its designated purpose. Make sure the additional funds are used for their intended purposes by considering:

■ the extent to which the funds are appropriately allocated;

■ how well the school monitors the effectiveness of the spending;

■ whether the outcomes of the expenditure match the objectives;

■ how well the use of additional grants relates to the school's provision, for example for teaching, curriculum and assessment.

☐ **The extent to which the principles of best value are applied in the school's use of resources**

To what extent are best value principles of comparison, challenge, consultation and competition applied in the school's management and use of resources?

Detailed guidance on the concepts embodied in best value principles can be found in Annex 1 of this *Handbook*. In all inspections the use the school makes of best value principles must be evaluated.

Schools applying best value principles will recognise the importance of questions such as:

■ How do our standards and costs **compare** with those of other schools?

■ How do we **challenge** ourselves to justify the use of resources to provide educational activities outside the statutory curriculum, for instance parent–school partnerships and vocational courses?

■ How do we satisfy ourselves that **competition** is fair where we buy contracted-out services, for instance school meals?

■ How widely do we **consult**, for example on major spending decisions and changes to the curriculum?

The answers to these questions will tell you how well the school is applying the best value principles.

Example 7.8

Extract from a full inspection report on a primary school

The governing body is shrewd and very effective, and is aware of best value principles. It takes a keen interest in the performance of the school and the way it is perceived locally. It makes very good use of detailed analysis of assessment results, including comparisons with other schools, to target its spending to bring about improvements in standards. The headteacher systematically asks staff at staff meetings to justify the balance of time spent in their classes on the foundation subjects in the National Curriculum. The school annually seeks the views of parents about possible changes to the curriculum for the following year and informs them of resulting decisions. The governing body invites formal tenders for building maintenance and has strict criteria for selecting contractors but did not seek competitive quotations the last time the school bought computers.

[Overall: very good application of best value principles (2)]

☐ **The adequacy of staffing, accommodation and learning resources, highlighting strengths and weaknesses in different subjects and areas of the curriculum where they affect the quality of education provided and the educational standards achieved**

Do the number, qualifications and experience of teachers and support staff match the demands of the curriculum?

In FULL INSPECTIONS only, evaluate the extent to which the school is staffed and resourced to teach the curriculum and whether there are any features that contribute to or detract from good quality and high standards. A good school makes the best use of all its available resources to achieve the highest possible standards for all its pupils.

Evaluate how far the staff are qualified to teach the school's curriculum, and are trained or experienced in the appropriate phase, and the extent to which levels of staffing ensure that all pupils are taught effectively. Consider whether there are enough skilled support staff to enable the school to function effectively. Take into account the qualifications and experience of those staff in relation to the needs of the pupils in the school. You should give particular attention to the effectiveness of the use of staff working with pupils who have special education needs and for whom English is an additional language.

When considering the adequacy of the **number, qualifications and experience of teachers and support staff** keep in mind that:

- in many schools, nursery assistants and other staff provide complementary support for the work of teachers;

- in an effective team all staff understand their role as well as those of others;

- staff should be trained and experienced to provide the appropriate age-related curriculum;

- every school should have a co-ordinator for special educational needs;

- additional support may be provided for some pupils with statements of special education need and for those for whom English is an additional language;

- a school that is a designated support base for pupils with statements will have prescribed staffing levels.

Where the school is affected by staff illness or a pattern of absence comes to your attention, you should evaluate what the school does to support staff and reduce staff absence.

Does the accommodation allow the curriculum to be taught effectively? Are learning resources adequate for the school's curriculum and range of pupils?

Your evaluation of the adequacy and effectiveness of accommodation and learning resources should be informed by particular strengths and weaknesses identified during the inspection. You should note where provision enhances or detracts from pupils' learning. Evaluate the quality of the accommodation, including outdoor areas, particularly for the younger pupils, and whether they provide a stimulating and well-maintained place for pupils to learn and play. Judge the adequacy and effectiveness of learning resources according to the level of provision, its appropriateness, condition and accessibility. You should judge the effectiveness of the library by the ways in which it promotes higher levels of literacy for all pupils; by the way it is a resource for personal study; by its contribution in encouraging pupils to read widely and confidently; and the extent to which pupils value reading as a source of pleasure and information. Make your judgements and record your **evidence only where provision has a significant impact on standards.**

8. WHAT SHOULD THE SCHOOL DO TO IMPROVE FURTHER?

The report must include:

☐ specific matters – key issues – which the appropriate authority for the school should include in its post-inspection action plan, listed as issues for action in order of their importance in raising standards in the school;

Each issue must be followed by a reference to the main paragraph(s) in the inspection report where the weaknesses are discussed.

These issues should be based on any weaknesses identified in the inspection and include all the matters listed in WHAT COULD BE IMPROVED in relation to **standards** achieved and the **quality of education** provided, with particular emphasis on **teaching**.

Where the inspection highlights issues already identified as priorities in the school's development plan, this section should acknowledge this.

Any non-compliance with statutory requirements where it detracts significantly from the quality and standards of the school, or where it relates to care, health and safety, should be reported here.

☐ a statement indicating paragraphs of the inspection report which refer to other weaknesses, not included in issues for action, but which should be considered by the school.

INSPECTION FOCUS

This section of the report is linked directly to the statements made in the summary under the heading WHAT COULD BE IMPROVED. In that section, you need to summarise the school's main weaknesses without, at that stage, giving the direction in which the school might move to bring about improvements. The statements included in WHAT SHOULD THE SCHOOL DO TO IMPROVE FURTHER? take that step. They set out what needs to be done to bring about improvement. However, you must not go further than this to indicate how the school could take the required action; that is the proper remit of the school's governors and staff. But you must make it absolutely clear what needs to be done, breaking down the statement into several parts if it helps to clarify what the school must do.

☐ **Specific matters – key issues – which the appropriate authority for the school should include in its post-inspection action plan, listed as issues for action in order of their importance in raising standards in the school**

Each bullet point in the section WHAT COULD BE IMPROVED must, one by one, be covered in this section so that the reader can immediately link each issue for action by the school to an inspection judgement. You must use this section to make it very clear to the school the steps they must take to bring about the improvement that you have identified. This means that you will almost certainly need to use a list format with a number of actions under a heading linked back to the bullet point in WHAT COULD BE IMPROVED.

These key issues should be the big issues for the school, and not matters which are less significant. The detail of this section must naturally lead the school to improvement. A compliance issue should only be included here if it detracts significantly from the quality of the school's provision or the standards that pupils attain. In a SHORT INSPECTION, the level of effectiveness of the school means that it is unlikely that there will be significant compliance issues, but if they do arise they should be indicated here. In a FULL INSPECTION, you should avoid making a long list of compliance issues here unless they are significant.

Example 8.1

Extracts from a primary inspection report

WHAT COULD BE IMPROVED

- *The teaching of mathematics in Key Stage 2*

- *The attainment of higher-achieving pupils in Years 3 and 5*

- *The effectiveness of monitoring teaching to identify what does or does not work well in lessons*

WHAT SHOULD THE SCHOOL DO TO IMPROVE FURTHER?

- *Improve the teaching of mathematics in Key Stage 2 so that it challenges all pupils and fully meets the National Curriculum requirements by:*

  - *increasing teachers' knowledge of data handling and algebra (paragraphs 7, 10, 36);*

  - *planning tasks which involve pupils in investigative approaches to learning mathematics (paragraphs 14, 15, 23, 28).*

- *Improve the attainment of high-attaining pupils in Years 3 and 5 by:*

  - *accurately assessing their attainment and using this information to develop a programme of work in each section which stretches these pupils further;*

  - *setting challenging learning goals in lessons for these pupils.*

- *Sharpen the evaluation of teaching and learning by:*

  - *having a clear focus when observing lessons and scrutinising pupils' work;*

  - *identifying what each teacher does well to promote successful learning;*

  - *agreeing where improvements are needed to make learning more effective.*

☐ **A statement indicating paragraphs of the report which refer to other weaknesses not included in issues for action, but which should be considered by the school**

In FULL INSPECTIONS, only you should use this statement to bring to the attention of the school those weaknesses which need to be considered by the school but which do not appear as one of the main areas for improvement. You should also use this statement to include compliance issues which, although important, do not significantly detract from the education pupils receive or the standards they achieve.

Example 8.2

Extracts from a primary inspection report

OTHER ISSUES WHICH SHOULD BE CONSIDERED BY THE SCHOOL

- *Completing the fragmented schemes of work in history, geography and art (paragraphs 25, 102, 105, 107)*

- *Extending and improving the amount of information given to parents about the curriculum (paragraph 35)*

- *Ensuring that child protection training for the newest members of staff is completed as soon as possible (paragraph 44)*

9. OTHER SPECIFIED FEATURES

Where additional features are specified for inspection, inspectors must evaluate and report on:

☐ the overall effectiveness of each feature.

In determining their judgements, inspectors should consider the extent to which:

- one or more specified criteria are met.

SCHOOL DATA AND INDICATORS

PART C OF THE INSPECTION REPORT

After OTHER SPECIFIED FEATURES, if any, the inspection report will contain data and indicators which are defined by the report template that is in use at the time of the inspection.

THE INSPECTION OF OTHER FEATURES

The inspection focus for any additional features for inspection, for example a survey of an issue in primary schools over a particular term, will be specified along with the feature itself.

Each feature specified will be accompanied by:

- an evaluation and reporting requirement indicated by ☐;

- up to three inspection criteria;

- a commentary covering the inspection focus;

- a summary of reporting requirements;

- guidance in the format of this *Handbook*, including sections on the inspection focus, making your judgement, and guidance on the inspection criteria.

10. THE STANDARDS AND QUALITY OF TEACHING IN AREAS OF THE CURRICULUM, SUBJECTS AND COURSES

FULL INSPECTIONS ONLY – PART D OF THE INSPECTION REPORT

Areas of learning (or the Foundation Curriculum for nursery and reception pupils)

The report must include evaluation of:

- [ ] the standards achieved, stating the extent to which pupils are on course to reach the expected outcomes or goals by 5 years and the quality of teaching in each area of learning;

- [ ] changes since the previous inspection;

- [ ] any other factors which have a bearing on what is achieved.

The report should highlight any differences in provision or attainment for pupils who are 5 or under in nursery, reception or mixed-age classes.

Subjects

For each subject, where evidence allows, the report should include evaluation of:

- [ ] standards of work in the subject, particularly the standards achieved by the oldest pupils in each Key Stage, highlighting what pupils do well and could do better;

- [ ] changes since the previous inspection;

- [ ] how well pupils are taught, highlighting effective and ineffective teaching in the subject and relating the demands made by teachers to pupils' learning and the progress they have made;

- [ ] any other factors which have a bearing on what is achieved, especially the extent to which management of the subject is directed towards monitoring, evaluating and improving performance.

In English and mathematics, the subject reports of work should draw on evidence of the contribution made by other subjects to pupils' competence in literacy and numeracy. In information and communications technology (ICT), the report should draw on evidence of contributions made to pupils' IT capability from all other subjects.

The report must include separate sections on English and mathematics. It should include sections on other subjects of the curriculum where there is sufficient evidence.

PART 2

GUIDANCE FOR INSPECTORS ON CONDUCTING INSPECTIONS AND WRITING REPORTS

INSPECTION QUALITY

1   This guidance will help you to interpret the inspection requirements set out in *Inspecting Schools*, the inspection Framework. It follows the sequence of work required before, during and after an inspection.

2   The guidance is for all inspectors and contractors. The registered inspector is ultimately responsible for the inspection and the report. This guidance therefore focuses particularly on his/her role. However, all inspectors in a team must work to the inspection requirements set out here, especially the Code of Conduct, and measure up to the Quality Guarantee for teachers. The inspection contractor has to meet OFSTED's Quality Assurance Standard as a condition for being awarded inspection work.

Setting a standard for inspection

3   As an inspector, you need to have high personal and professional qualities. When inspecting, you should treat all the people you meet – pupils, parents, staff, governors and others – as you would expect them to treat you, with interest, courtesy and respect. You should regard your right of entry to schools as a privilege.

4   Assessing the professional competence of others can arouse anxieties. Inspection is no exception. You must see to it that you recognise and praise strengths as well as probe areas of weakness. You must be alert to the sensitivities of staff but also be objective in all you do.

5   There are four main strands to inspection:

   ■ finding out what the school is like, and its strengths and weaknesses;

   ■ diagnosing what makes it the way it is;

   ■ identifying what it needs to do next to improve;

   ■ reflecting these findings back to the school, both orally and in the written inspection report.

6   Inspection is effective when it is seen by schools as fair, rigorous and helpful. The school must respect and value the quality and expertise of the inspection team. If it does, it will accept and make use of the inspection's findings to help it move forward. Otherwise, the usefulness of inspection is greatly reduced.

7   Inspection, therefore, must not only arrive at the right judgements but also be done in the right way.

Quality Guarantee for schools

8   We attach such a high priority to the effect of inspection on schools, that we expect all inspectors actively to reflect and promote the Quality Guarantee we give to teachers.

QUALITY GUARANTEE

- *Inspectors will do everything possible to work with you in keeping the stress of an inspection to a minimum.*

- *Inspectors will not expect you to create additional paperwork specifically for the inspection.*

- *Inspectors will always treat you in a courteous and friendly manner, particularly when entering and leaving your classroom.*

- *Normally, you will be observed teaching for no more than half of any one day, and never more than three-quarters.*

- *Inspectors will not judge teaching unless they have observed a significant part of the lesson, normally for at least 30 minutes.*

- *Inspectors will use confidential information responsibly.*

- *Inspectors will discuss important aspects of your teaching with you.*

- *Inspectors will explain the reasons for their judgements and be helpful in identifying where improvement is needed.*

---

9   Most inspectors reflect these principles naturally in their work. The great majority of the responses we receive from teachers and schools show that most inspectors have high standards of conduct and professionalism.

10   But there are exceptions. There is no place for inspectors who are remote from the teachers, brusque, overbearing in their behaviour, or insensitive. Nor should you ask the school for paperwork it does not normally use, such as lesson plans to a particular format.

OFSTED's expectations of inspectors

11   Our expectations of inspectors are set out in the Framework and include the following.

12   **You must be thoroughly prepared for the inspection and understand the context of the school and its pupils.** It takes time to prepare properly. You should ensure that the contractor gives you enough time. If you are a registered inspector, the quality of your *Pre-Inspection Commentary* is vital. If the issues it identifies are clear, and you brief your team well, the inspection will get off to a good start.

13   **You must have thorough knowledge and understanding of the Framework, this *Inspection Handbook*, the subjects and aspects you inspect and the age range of the pupils concerned.** You work in a changing educational scene. Curriculum requirements change, as do the national policies. You must keep yourself up to date. This means consulting documents from various sources: from OFSTED, the DfEE, the Qualifications and Curriculum Authority (QCA) and other relevant bodies. To inspect English in a primary school, you should have a thorough knowledge of teaching the skills of literacy and of the National Literacy Strategy. Only then will you be able to

judge unequivocally how effective a school's own literacy strategy is. Equally, those who enter the world of 3- or 4-year-olds must be thoroughly conversant with the needs of these young children, the curriculum framework which applies to them, and what makes for good teaching.

14 **You must uphold the highest professional standards required by the Code of Conduct, thus securing OFSTED's Quality Guarantee to teachers (*see above*).**

CODE OF CONDUCT

15 The Code of Conduct has been revised. To meet its principles, you must:

- **evaluate the work of the school objectively, be impartial and have no previous connection with the school, its staff or governors which could undermine your objectivity;**

   We take the questions of impartiality and connection seriously. If you have had anything to do with the school in the past few years, you should consider carefully whether you should be part of the school's inspection team. You should certainly rule yourself out if this contact included any 'pre-inspection' work, staff appointments, advice or staff development. If in doubt, you should err on the side of caution. If you are a team inspector you must, as a condition of your enrolment, inform the registered inspector and contractor of any connection at all with the school.

- **report honestly and fairly, ensuring that judgements accurately and reliably reflect what the school achieves and does;**

   Judgements must be robust and fully supported by evidence so that you can defend them, if required. They must be accurate and carefully weighed and tested against the inspection criteria. They must also be reliable, which means that other trained inspectors, using the same evidence, would be highly likely to come to the same judgement.

- **carry out your work with integrity, treating all those you meet with courtesy and sensitivity;**

   It is important that you leave staff feeling as though they have been treated well and fairly.

- **do all you can to minimise stress, in particular by ensuring that no teacher is over-inspected and by not asking for paperwork to be specifically prepared for the inspection;**

   We are committed to reducing stress among teachers as far as possible. Inspectors must do everything they can to allay anxiety. This must start from the moment they begin to have dealings with the school and continue until the report is published. Teachers are naturally apprehensive about inspection. We expect you to do what you can to put them at their ease. There are clear guidelines about how much teachers should be observed during a day. If you are the registered inspector, we expect you to ensure that these guidelines are followed.

- **act with the best interests and well-being of pupils and staff as priorities;**

   The deal the pupils get is at the heart of your work. It is essential that you discover their views of the school as well as evaluating their educational progress and achievements. You must certainly not cause pupils any anxiety. You have many dealings with them during an inspection. Your questioning should not make them feel vulnerable or inadequate. Your relations with them must be a model of propriety. You must not put them in a position where they may feel conflicting loyalties.

■ **communicate with staff purposefully and productively, and present your judgements of the school's work clearly and frankly;**

In your dealings with teachers, you should build confidence and mutual respect. You should seek to understand what they are doing and why, and share with them your views about what you find. We cannot stress enough the importance of feeding back your findings in a helpful way.

■ **respect the confidentiality of information, particularly about teachers and the judgements made about their individual teaching.**

In judging teaching, you are undertaking a form of professional appraisal. You should not criticise the work of a teacher, or anyone else involved with the school, within earshot of someone else. You should relay concerns to the headteacher or appropriate manager, but not before discussing them with the teacher concerned. Do not allow yourself to be placed in a position where you cannot use information you are given in the way you think best. At times, you may need to make it clear that you reserve the right to do as you see fit with certain information or evidence.

THE RECORD OF INSPECTION EVIDENCE

16   The record of evidence comprises:

i.   forms completed by the school:

- *Form S1*, consultation with the appropriate authority about the specification for the inspection, and data about the school;

- *Form S2*, further data about the school;

- *Form S3*, school self-audit;

- *Form S4*, school monitoring and self-evaluation;

ii. the *PICSI report* supplied by OFSTED;

iii. documentary evidence from the school (normally returned to the school after the inspection) and the previous inspection report;

iv. evidence and judgements recorded by inspectors, including:

- *Pre-Inspection Commentary*, with issues for inspection;

- *Evidence Forms*;

- *Inspection Notebooks* – one is completed by each member of the team on FULL INSPECTIONS (optional in SHORT INSPECTIONS);

- the *Record of Corporate Judgements*;

- evidence from parents.

17   Further details of the record of evidence are given in the sections which follow. Instructions for their completion are summarised in Annex 3.

EFFICIENT AND EFFECTIVE INSPECTION

18   The process of inspection, like developing a photographic image, is the progressive unveiling of the school until its essential character can be seen. As each part of the picture is revealed the image becomes clearer. Because inspection is such a concentrated process, from the start it must use all the evidence available to hypothesise about the school's quality and standards, and its potential strengths and weaknesses. This gives a focus for the inspectors' work.

19   However, inspection is not a mere snapshot of a school. The quality and standards of each school in England are now documented in one or more previous inspection reports. Each school's performance has been measured, year after year. The school's own planning also reflects its changing priorities and needs. Each school has an ongoing record, showing where it has come from: a performance trail.

THE INSPECTION SEQUENCE

20   The registered inspector should take full account of the recent history of the school's quality and standards, particularly when gauging the extent of improvement. Much of the information needed is presented in the *Pre-Inspection Context and School Indicator (PICSI) report*. Most schools have detailed performance data to augment the *PICSI* indicators.

21   You should also note what the school does to monitor and evaluate its own performance and what its evaluation shows. The inspection forms the school complete reflect the wish of many schools for inspectors to take self-evaluation into account.[1] *Form S3* invites the school to make its own assessment of compliance with statutory requirements: a self-audit. *Form S4* invites the school to present its own view of how it stands in relation to each of the areas of its work to be inspected. Using inspection to test the school's perceptions of itself gives an insight into how well it is managed. Inspection thus provides a mirror for the school.

22   The first stage of pre-inspection analysis should provide early hypotheses to follow up at the preliminary visit to the school. This visit should give you, as the registered inspector, a very helpful first impression of the *quality* of the school. It may be difficult for some headteachers to be available for discussion during the school day. In very small primary schools it may be possible for them to make arrangements for their classes to be covered for part of the time should this be necessary. By meeting the headteacher, staff, governors and pupils, and by looking round the school, you will get an important contextual picture to set alongside the data and documentary evidence.

23   You should now be in a position to complete most of the *Pre-Inspection Commentary* for the rest of the inspection team. Ideally this should take into account the views of parents, although this may depend on the timing of the parents' meeting. Your analysis must identify important issues and lines of enquiry for the inspection. Some of these may relate to apparent areas of strength or weakness, others to:

---

[1] This was also recommended by the Education and Employment Committee of the House of Commons, Fourth Report, *The Work of OFSTED*, London 1999.

- issues for action identified in the last inspection;

- claims made by the school in its self-evaluation report;

- features that relate to the school's particular circumstances;

- areas identified by the headteacher for inspection.

Above all, the issues must be specific to the school.

24   The *Pre-Inspection Commentary* has three purposes. First, it forms the basis for briefing other members of the team so that they know a great deal about the school when they arrive to start the inspection. Secondly, it provides an agenda of inspection priorities. Thirdly, it contributes to the judgements for the inspection report.

25   As the inspection progresses, there is often a change in emphasis, from establishing what the standards are and how well they reflect the earlier data, to securing explanations of why the achievements of the school are as they are. The quality of teaching will be an early focus.

26   At the end of the inspection, there should be a clear and shared view among the whole inspection team of the overall quality and standards of the school. In other words, how good it is. You should evaluate against each of the main requirements of the inspection schedule, and the team should reach a consensus view on the school's strengths, any areas for improvement, and what the school needs to do to improve. This process is summarised below.

The inspection sequence

Before the inspection   During the inspection   At the end of the inspection

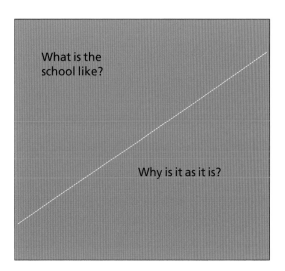

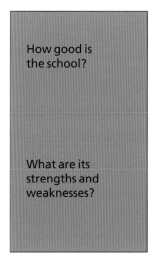

Pre-inspection analysis provides an initial view of the standards and possible quality of the school, influenced by visiting the school and hearing the views of the parents.

Initial emphasis on verifying the standards of the school and evaluating the quality of its provision. As the inspection proceeds, the relative impact of different factors is assessed.

Inspectors agree their judgements about standards, quality, strengths and weaknesses, focusing on teaching, leadership and management.

Finally they identify what the school should do to improve.

BEFORE THE INSPECTION

NOTICE OF INSPECTION

27 OFSTED has reduced the notice of inspection given to schools to between six and ten school weeks. The purpose of this is to reduce the pressure on teachers and other staff, and to avoid long, drawn-out processes, such as re-writing documents and making other preparations which some schools have felt they needed to do. The shorter notice has been welcomed by most schools. However, it does put some pressure on the school to complete the inspection forms on time, and on the contractor and registered inspector to make the necessary arrangements for the inspection.

28 The shorter notice of inspection places a premium on efficient procedures in the run-up to inspection. The inspection will take place during a five-week 'inspection window'. The possible sequence of pre-inspection events is illustrated below. The first five steps are fixed by the 'inspection window'; the rest will vary slightly in timing, depending on the date of the inspection.

Summary of pre-inspection steps

Six school weeks before the 'inspection window' (typically eight weeks before the inspection)	1. School receives notification of inspection, and whether this will be SHORT or FULL, a set of inspection forms, and a copy of the *PICSI report*	
Five school weeks before the inspection window (typically seven weeks before the inspection)	2. School returns *Form S1* to OFSTED	3. Contractor receives specification and *PICSI report* from OFSTED with *Form S1* and sets date of inspection with school and registered inspector 4. Registered inspector contacts school
Two school weeks before the inspection window (typically four weeks before the inspection)		5. Contractor sends outline inspection plan to OFSTED and item list to OFSTED and the school
Four weeks before the inspection	6. School sends *Forms S2–S4*, plus previous inspection report, prospectus and development plan to registered inspector and calls meeting for parents	7. Registered inspector receives documents from school, and prepares for visit
Two or three weeks before the inspection		8. Registered inspector visits school 9. Registered inspector plans the inspection in detail
Two weeks before the inspection		10. Registered inspector meets parents 11. Registered inspector completes *Pre-Inspection Commentary*
Before the inspection begins		12. Registered inspector meets and briefs team

STEPS 1 AND 2: INSPECTION SPECIFICATION

29   As soon as the school is notified of the inspection and whether it is to be SHORT or FULL, it is asked to complete *Form S1* and return it to OFSTED within one week. At the same time, OFSTED supplies the school with *Forms S2, S3* and *S4*, which the school has three weeks to complete in electronic or hardcopy format.

30   *Form S1* allows the appropriate authority to provide basic information about the nature and composition of the school. *Form S1* is used to draw up the specification which OFSTED issues to the contractor as part of the contract for inspection; it will help the contractor to determine the composition of the inspection team.

STEP 3: SETTING THE DATE

31   Once it has the specification, the contractor should move immediately to let the school know who is to be the registered inspector, and to establish the date of the inspection with the school and the registered inspector.

STEP 4: COMMUNICATING WITH THE SCHOOL AND PARENTS

32   If you are the registered inspector for the inspection, you should make contact with the headteacher of the school and:

- introduce yourself;

- find out how the headteacher, staff and governors are viewing the forthcoming inspection;

- enquire about progress in completing the *Forms S2–S4* and arrange for them to be *sent to you*, together with the other prescribed documents (*see paragraph 34*);

- arrange a date and time to visit the school, explaining what you wish to do during the visit, and set up a programme for it;

- discuss and agree dates and times for other events, including the parents' meeting, feedback to senior management team and governing body or appropriate authority, the period over which the school can check the draft report, and the days the inspection will last;

- check that the school has received the *PICSI report* from OFSTED;

- make the CVs of the inspection team available to the school.

STEPS 5, 6 AND 7: INITIAL PREPARATION

33   To make the most of your visit to the school you must prepare thoroughly. Contractors must make sure that time is provided for this.

34 You first need to assemble the core documents required before the visit. These are:

- *Form S1*, completed by the school and sent to you by OFSTED;

- *Forms S2, S3* and *S4* completed and sent to you by the school;

- the *PICSI report*, provided by OFSTED;

- the last inspection report, provided by the school;

- the current school development or management plan, provided by the school;

- the school prospectus or brochure, provided by the school.

35 You must not require any other documents from the school at this stage. The school has enough to do in completing the four forms, calling the parents' meeting and communicating with governors. Remember that the inspection must do everything possible to avoid putting an extra burden on schools or significantly affecting their normal patterns of work.

36 Your analysis of indicators and documents should be systematic and your enquiries related to the questions posed in the inspection *Schedule*. WHAT SORT OF SCHOOL IS IT? is both the starting point and the finishing point for your inspection. Start with the school's view of itself, expressed in its prospectus. Look at how it presents itself and what it considers to be important. Consider the extent to which pupils' interests are at the centre of the school's presentation and aspirations.

37 *Forms S1* and *S2* indicate who the pupils are, their background, mobility, home language and special educational needs. Look for evidence of effectiveness. Look at the pattern of the school's results, trends over time, high and low spots, and comparative data. Look at other indications of effectiveness, such as how the budget is constructed; the pattern of exclusions, if there are any; and attendance.

38 Then your analysis can move from outcomes to the quality of provision. Look at the curriculum as expressed qualitatively in the prospectus and quantitatively on *Form S2*. Consider whether it is giving the range of experiences you might expect, across the age range. Consider staffing and class organisation, the staff profile and deployment, and possible management issues. Look for the school's priorities for improvement reflected in the development plan.

39 After this analysis you should have a useful but partial picture of the school. This will include hypotheses that you will need to investigate further. What does this picture add up to? Where has the school come from and where is it heading? What appear to be the big issues in the school? What are the school's targets and is it likely to meet them? Three strong pieces of evidence are: the previous inspection report; the headteacher's evaluation report on *Form S4*; and the *PICSI report*.

40 By putting the information from these different sources together, you should be able to: estimate how the school is performing; know what its priorities now are; see whether these have changed since the last inspection; and consider how the school views its own quality and standards. You will have an initial impression of the school which will form the basis for discussion when you meet the headteacher.

41   You are now in a position to begin to write the *Pre-Inspection Commentary*, which you will add to significantly and complete after the preliminary visit to the school. You should include views about:

■ standards attained in the core subjects of English, mathematics and science, highlighting any patterns of strengths or weaknesses;

■ any trends in attainment over time, where appropriate;

■ whether or not, according to quantitative indicators, the school has improved since its last inspection;

■ areas that might need further exploration during the inspection;

■ the quality of management.

STEP 8: VISITING THE SCHOOL

42   The visit to the school is a very important part of the inspection process and is likely to last for a day. It has five main purposes:

i.   to establish a good and trusting working relationship between you (the registered inspector) and the school, particularly the headteacher;

ii.   to gain a better understanding of the school, its nature, what it is aiming to do and how it goes about its work;

iii.   to consider aspects of the school on which inspectors might focus, some of which may be identified by the school;

iv.   to brief the staff and any governors who are able to meet you on how the inspection will work;

v.   to agree the necessary arrangements for the inspection.

43   To achieve these intentions you will need to plan the visit carefully, in consultation with the headteacher. Where the headteacher has charge of a class, or has a nursery school, her/his availability may be limited to after school hours, unless cover can be arranged. There is no imperative, however, for the school to arrange cover, nor should you expect it.

44   Ideally, you will need to do the following during the initial visit:

■ have an extensive discussion with the headteacher to find out more about the school and the way it is run, and to test your initial perceptions; and tour the school, to become acquainted with its geography, if possible meeting some pupils and staff;

■ meet the staff of the school, to brief them on how the inspection will be organised and respond to any queries they may have;

■ meet any representatives of the governing body, again to discuss the inspection with them, but also to learn how the governing body has been involved with developments since the last inspection, and how it perceives its current role and priorities. You should arrange to meet governors during the inspection as well.

45 Your meetings with the headteacher, staff and governors should put them at their ease by explaining how the inspection will be run, and give them confidence in the process. They should be helped to see how they can gain value from it. You should explain:

For a SHORT INSPECTION

- how the SHORT INSPECTION can only be a light 'health check' of the school, not an intensive subject-by-subject inspection;

- the basis for sampling lessons, with the possibility that some teachers or subjects will not be seen;

- that inspectors will discuss work with teachers as they go, giving whatever feedback they can;

- that the report will focus on the main strengths of the school and areas needing improvement.

For a FULL INSPECTION

- that a significant amount of every teacher's work will be seen, including, in a primary school, their teaching of the literacy hour and numeracy sessions;

- how all teachers will be offered feedback on their work and receive their profile of lesson grades.

46 Discuss with the headteacher the arrangements for the parents' meeting. Discuss whether the school can provide a room for the inspection team to work in during the inspection. If the school is unable to do this without disturbing its own work, the inspectors will have to make their own arrangements for a base.

47 During the preliminary visit, you should request from the school any additional documents which will be needed in advance of the inspection. These must be those which the school already has, or can easily supply. You should not ask the headteacher to prepare additional documents specifically for the inspection. To make the inspection run smoothly, you will need:

- a programme, or timetable, of the school's work in the period of the inspection;

- a staff handbook, if one is available, or list of staff responsibilities and/or objectives;

- a plan of the school.

48 In a FULL INSPECTION, you will need to take away, or see at a later stage, further documents such as:

- the governors' annual report to parents;

- minutes of the meetings of the governing body, or the equivalent where the 'appropriate authority' is not the governing body;

- evidence of progress towards the targets set by governors;

- curriculum plans, policies, guidelines or schemes of work already in existence;

- the outcomes of self-evaluations carried out recently by the school;

- the outcomes of any external monitoring and evaluations carried out since the last inspection;

- any other documentation the school wishes you to consider, subject to your agreement.

You should return all of these to the school after the inspection.

49   In a SHORT INSPECTION, you should avoid taking further documentation away from the school. You should not ask the school to collect together curriculum plans, policies, guidelines or schemes of work, no matter how important the school feels they are. Only if specific issues arise during the inspection, where the reasons for a particular strength or weakness need be explored, should you ask to see any related material.

50   There is a lot of ground to cover on the preliminary visit; therefore it is not ideal to hold the parents' meeting on the same day.

STEP 9: PLANNING THE INSPECTION

51   The registered inspector should:

- ensure responsibilities are assigned for all subjects and aspects, special educational needs, equal opportunities; and, where relevant, children under 5 and English as an additional language;

- decide the deployment of the team on the basis of a clear strategy for sampling the work of the school, taking account of the areas of expertise of team members;

- plan the deployment of inspectors, particularly on the first day, and ensure that each inspector has an appropriate schedule of inspection activities to cover in addition to his/her responsibilities;

- plan to collect evidence relating to particular aspects identified as focal points in the *Pre-Inspection Commentary*;

- plan, in conjunction with the school, when discussions with staff will take place and, on FULL INSPECTIONS, agree when the feedback to subject co-ordinators and classroom teachers will be held;

- in SHORT INSPECTIONS, decide whether or not *Inspection Notebooks* will be used;

- set deadlines for team inspectors to complete *Inspection Notebooks* (remember that, apart from the draft sections for the report, these must be completed before the final team meeting);

- in FULL INSPECTIONS, set deadlines for team inspectors to submit draft sections for the report.

STEP 10: MEETING WITH PARENTS

52   The pre-inspection meeting with parents is a legal requirement. The meeting must take place before the inspection begins so that the registered inspector can fully consider the parents' views as important pre-inspection evidence. Parents should have as much notice of the meeting as possible. The 'appropriate authority' (usually the governing body) is responsible for organising the meeting. Only parents or carers of pupils registered at the school should be invited. The headteacher or one of the governors, usually the chair, may introduce you to the parents at the meeting. Any member of staff, or governor, who is also a parent or carer of a pupil at the school may attend the meeting. OFSTED provides a sample letter of invitation and the suggested agenda for the meeting (available on the CD-ROM attached to this *Handbook*).

53   The registered inspector should invite the governing body to distribute the standard questionnaire to parents (available on the CD-ROM). Individual responses are confidential to the inspection team and there should be arrangements to ensure that this is the case. Inspection contractors have translations of the questionnaire in the more commonly used home languages and at an early stage you should check with the school whether these are needed. If forms in other languages are used, you will need to plan to have comments translated.

54   The school should distribute the questionnaire on the basis of one per pupil. However, its normal procedures should be used where information is sent separately to more than one person with responsibility for the child, making sure that sufficient questionnaires are sent so that parents can respond separately for each child.

55   You should base the meeting on the standard agenda for parents' meetings (available on the CD-ROM) and give parents the opportunity to express their views on:

■ the standards the school achieves;

■ how the school helps pupils, whatever their ability, to learn and make progress;

■ the attitudes and values the school promotes;

■ behaviour and attendance;

■ the work the school expects pupils to do at home; and the school's links with parents, including information on how pupils are getting on;

■ how the school responds to parents' suggestions and concerns;

■ how the school has improved in recent years.

56   You should also invite views on any other matters which the parents may wish to raise. You should ask parents not to name individual pupils and teachers at any stage during the meeting. You should explain in general terms the forthcoming inspection and its purpose. You may need to explain why the school has been selected for a particular type of inspection.

57   As soon as possible after the meeting is over, and you have received the returned questionnaires and analysed them, you should discuss with the headteacher the significant issues and concerns raised by parents. You should give the headteacher the opportunity to offer you other evidence of parents' views about the school. You should explain that the inspectors' views on what parents say about the school will form part of the feedback at the end of the inspection, and also will be contained in the written report.

STEP 11: COMPLETION OF THE *PRE-INSPECTION COMMENTARY*

58   After the visit to the school, you should be in a position to prepare a detailed, well-informed and penetrating *Pre-Inspection Commentary* on the school. This commentary should be completed for as many sections of the schedule as possible.

59   You should give preliminary views about:

- the characteristics of the school;

- standards, trends in attainment, and improvement since the last inspection, adding to your existing commentary on these areas;

- attendance and exclusions, with potential views on attitudes and behaviour;

- the match of staff expertise to subjects taught and any implications for attainment shown in the data;

- the range and quality of the school's educational provision and other aspects of the school, making full use of the school's documents provided.

60   You should present initial hypotheses about why the standards achieved are as they are and any significant variation over time and between subjects or groups of pupils. You should highlight in particular those features of the school that appear to impact on standards, such as:

- possible changes in the quality of teaching caused by staff turnover, monitoring and evaluation strategies, or in-service training;

- features of the school's context and organisation such as mixed-aged classes;

- the impact of the school's context and its leadership and management;

- changes in curriculum provision, such as the introduction of the National Literacy and Numeracy strategies;

- the use of resources to promote standards.

61   These are matters that you must pursue in the inspection. You should also form hypotheses about:

- the extent, and adequacy, of the school's improvement since the last inspection;

- whether the school might be underachieving, have serious weaknesses, or require special measures.

62   In considering the pre-inspection information, do not lose sight of the wood for the trees. Ensure that the *Pre-Inspection Commentary* paints the 'big picture' of the school, and that the central hypotheses about the school stand out clearly. Effective *Pre-Inspection Commentaries* for both SHORT and FULL INSPECTIONS:

- draw on the full range of pre-inspection evidence, including the school's self-evaluation, views formed during the pre-inspection visit, parents' views and returned questionnaires;

- make full use of the *PICSI* data and the comparative figures in the *PICSI* annexes;

- build substantially on the issues raised in the previous inspection report; and the school's actions in response to them;

- provide an accurate historical analysis of the school's achievements and trends;

- identify hypotheses for further exploration or confirmation: issues for inspection.

STEP 12: TEAM BRIEFING AND MEETING

63   The team should meet for a final briefing before starting the inspection. You should note that:

- this is more than a short gathering before the first morning's inspection begins. A thorough briefing is required;

- it could be a morning meeting prior to beginning the inspection in the afternoon, or a separate meeting before the first day of the inspection;

- the meeting must not encroach on inspection time;

- the meeting should be for the whole inspection team, and where any team member begins the inspection at a later stage, arrangements must be made for a thorough briefing at that stage.

64   As the registered inspector, you will check the background and strengths of the team, if you do not already know them, and then:

- brief the team about the school and the *Pre-Inspection Commentary*;

- alert the team to any concerns or anxieties felt by the school or staff;

- ensure that all members of the team gather evidence against all the schedule headings;

- ensure that all members of the team know exactly what their first day's programme is to be;

- on FULL INSPECTIONS, ensure they have completed their subject *Pre-Inspection Commentaries*;

- clarify organisation and administrative arrangements;

- ensure that all are clear about their expected conduct.

65   You should make sure that the team is aware of all the issues and how these are to be tracked through. But above all, inspectors need to be aware of the 'big issues'. For example, if there is a strong boy/girl difference in test results, this should be clearly stated so that inspectors reflect their relative performance in each *Evidence Form* they write. The team should understand the school almost as well as you do by the end of the briefing.

DURING THE INSPECTION

THE ROLE OF THE REGISTERED INSPECTOR

66   As the registered inspector, you are the manager of the inspection team and the whole inspection process, and the first point of reference for everyone involved in the inspection. Effective management and organisation of the team on a day-to-day basis are crucial to the success of the inspection. It is your responsibility to ensure that judgements about the school are fair and accurate, are based on secure and representative evidence, comprehensively cover the schedule and contract requirements, and are corporately agreed. You are responsible for drawing key judgements together in the *Record of Corporate Judgements*.

67   You should:

- ensure that inspectors are consistent in their approaches to collecting and recording evidence and in how they conduct themselves and provide feedback to teachers;

- be prepared to adjust the patterns of work of individual inspectors as circumstances dictate;

- monitor and, if necessary, intervene in the work of the team to ensure compliance with the Framework and secure the necessary quality of evidence and judgements;

- undertake direct inspection such as observing work in classrooms, sampling pupils' written work, and holding discussions with staff, governors and pupils;

- keep a careful check on the sampling of the school's work and the extent of observation of individual teachers.

TEAM INSPECTORS' ASSIGNMENTS

68   Inspectors need to plan and use their time carefully and efficiently to achieve the coverage required, but they should be sensitive to the impact of the inspection on teachers and other staff in the school. Inspecting and evaluating the following aspects of the school's work will require contributions from the whole team but will need to be co-ordinated by one inspector:

- the quality of provision for pupils with special educational needs and the standards achieved by them;

- equality of opportunity for different groups of pupils;

- pupils' spiritual, moral, social and cultural development.

69   In FULL INSPECTIONS, inspectors need to draw evidence relating to their subject from across the curriculum. So, for example, the inspector co-ordinating the inspection of English will need to take account of pupils' competence in reading, writing, speaking and listening, and of opportunities for developing these competencies in subjects other than English. This will require other inspectors to contribute. The same is true for mathematics, in relation to numeracy skills, and information technology. In these cases, the inspector taking the lead will need evidence from across the curriculum.

70 Team meetings are an essential part of any inspection. They allow contributions from all inspectors and generate a sense of common purpose based on good working relationships, and a clear understanding of everyone's responsibilities within the team. As the registered inspector, you should structure and manage these meetings to provide opportunities for:

- the proper consideration and exchange of inspection evidence and inspectors' views;

- discussion of emerging issues which require the attention of the whole team;

- the resolution of issues for inspection identified in the *Pre-Inspection Commentary*;

- discussion of any gaps or weaknesses in the evidence base and how to fill them;

- debate about evidence, views and judgements to ensure consistency and to resolve any conflicts where they arise.

71 It is good practice to establish a programme of team meetings with clear agendas before the inspection begins. You will need to build in some flexibility to take account of any emerging issues during the inspection. Team meetings must not encroach on inspection time.

GATHERING THE INSPECTION EVIDENCE

72 Within their assignments on FULL INSPECTIONS, individual inspectors must be allocated time to collect the range of evidence on which the judgements of the team must be based. They must also ensure they have enough evidence to form judgements in their own subjects. The evidence includes:

- the inspection of teaching and of pupils at work in classrooms and other areas; and work off-site where the inspection priorities allow, where there is agreement with the 'appropriate authority', and where it is practicable and manageable;

- discussions with pupils, for example, to assess their understanding and knowledge of different subjects and their attitudes to work and their life at school;

- the analysis of samples of pupils' work within individual subjects and across the curriculum;

- discussions with staff, especially those with management responsibilities, such as subject or Key Stage co-ordinators;

- documentary analysis of schemes of work and teachers' plans, together with records of National Curriculum tests and teachers' assessments, any assessment undertaken of attainment on entry, and other measures or indicators of attainment and progress used by the school;

- the analysis of statements of special educational needs, annual and transitional reviews and individual education plans.

73 The evidence should be recorded on *Evidence Forms* and summarised in *Inspection Notebooks* as the inspection proceeds.

74   In SHORT INSPECTIONS, **all** inspectors will collect evidence, mainly from observation of lessons, across all relevant parts of the *Evaluation Schedule*. Individual inspectors will be assigned during the inspection to follow up particular issues, often through discussions, and will need to report these back to the rest of the team at team meetings. You should try to avoid undertaking too much documentary analysis in a SHORT INSPECTION. Confine this to those areas where there are particular strengths or weaknesses, to follow up why things are the way they are. The evidence should be recorded on *Evidence Forms*. If you choose to do so, you can use *Inspection Notebooks* to help you record your views and judgements and to structure your contribution to team meetings.

OBSERVATION OF LESSONS AND OTHER ACTIVITIES

75   While the school is in session the inspection team should aim to spend at least 60 per cent of its time observing lessons and sampling pupils' work. The time spent in lessons will vary, but some whole lessons must be observed, particularly literacy hours and numeracy sessions, if the school operates these. Lessons or sessions observed should be from the school's normal programme of work. Inspectors should not require changes to that programme.

76   In SHORT INSPECTIONS the sample of lessons should provide a cross-section of the work of the school. You should focus on the beginnings and ends of Key Stages, in particular Years 2/3 and 6, and the oldest children under 5. You should select the sample to include observation of the teaching of those teachers who hold management and/or curricular responsibility, for example:

   ■ the headteacher if he/she is in charge of a class or has a significant teaching load;

   ■ the deputy headteacher;

   ■ English and mathematics co-ordinators teaching their subject (or a literacy hour, for example);

   ■ those responsible for the early years and Key Stages.

77   In FULL INSPECTIONS lesson observations should include sufficient work in each Key Stage. Inspectors should spend enough time in lessons to enable them to make valid and reliable judgements on standards, teaching and learning. There should be a particular focus on the attainment of the oldest pupils. You must ensure that each teacher present in the school during the inspection is observed at least once and should aim to observe every class teacher teaching at least one whole or part lesson of English and mathematics.

78   In nursery schools, classes or units, you should observe the oldest and youngest children, recording your evidence for these groups on separate *Evidence Forms*. In mixed-age classes you should, as far as possible, also record the evidence for different age groups on separate forms.

79   In the smallest schools, the team may consist only of the registered inspector and the lay inspector, spending one day in the school. Small schools face particular challenges and you will need to evaluate how well they are met. For example:

• the class, or classes, cater for a wide age range	• raises questions about the match of work to pupils' needs and providing appropriate challenges and resources for all, particularly if there are nursery-aged children as well
• pupils may remain in one class for three, four or more years	• raises questions about whether the curriculum is planned to cover several years, avoiding repetition and retaining freshness, breadth and progression
• teaching staff may lack expertise in one or more curriculum areas	• raises questions about how the school redresses this
• pupils, particularly at the ends of Key Stages, may have few peers of the same age or capability	• raises questions about whether the school makes any arrangements to compensate for social and intellectual isolation
• there may only be a few nursery-aged children for certain days of the week	• raises the question of how appropriate are the school's curriculum, equipment and spaces for young children

80   Effective inspection involves joining individual pupils to look at their work and to discuss it with them. It also entails careful observation of teaching, including the organisation of work for pupils as a class, in groups or individually. Both need to be done so as not to disrupt either teaching or learning, and the taking of notes should be as unobtrusive as possible.

81   The load on teachers should be spread as evenly as possible. Wherever possible, teachers should not be kept waiting for their first visit from an inspector until near the end of the inspection. Inspectors should visit classes taught by supply teachers who are in the school for more than one day, and trainee teachers.

82   There should not normally be more than one inspector in a class at any time unless the class teacher agrees and there is a particular reason for it. An example would be to track the progress of a pupil with special educational needs, or where the registered inspector monitors the work of team members.

83   Inspection should include assemblies, extra-curricular activities, including sport if offered, and registration periods. It may also include fieldwork and educational visits where justifiable and practicable.

TALKING WITH PUPILS

84   Talking to pupils is a good source of evidence about what they know, can do and understand. It is particularly helpful in judging the extent of their understanding of current and recent work, and their ability to apply knowledge in different contexts. These discussions should take place as inspectors join individual pupils or groups of pupils at work in lessons. You should also use every opportunity to talk to pupils outside lessons, to find out their views of the school, their attitudes, their interests and the extent to which these are supported or fulfilled.

85   In all observation, it is important to listen to pupils':

   ■ incidental talk and comments;

   ■ contributions in class;

   ■ responses to questions;

   ■ questions, initiated by them;

   ■ views, feelings and comments expressed in discussions.

THE ANALYSIS OF PUPILS' WORK

86   Pupils' earlier and current work provides an essential source of evidence of their attainment and progress. It also offers an insight into the curriculum, teaching and pupils' attitudes to work. You will need to look at samples of work. The nature of the samples should be agreed with the headteacher during the preliminary visit.

87   It is helpful if the analysis takes place near the beginning of the inspection. Importantly, it will help the team to form an early view of the standards achieved. In English, mathematics and science, the review and analysis of pupils' work need to establish whether the standards of the oldest pupils in each Key Stage mirror what the performance data show. This will help you to see what pupils do well and not so well.

88   In SHORT INSPECTIONS the sample should include:

   ■ a sample of individual pieces of work in English and mathematics, selected by the school and drawn from across year groups to illustrate the standards achieved by the school and how pupils' work develops over time;

   ■ a representative sample of the work of all pupils with statements of special educational needs.

89   In FULL INSPECTIONS, the sample should include:

   ■ the work of pupils in all year groups in all subjects. The sample in each year should include two pupils from each group of pupils of above-average, average and below-average attainment;

   ■ the work of all pupils with statements of special educational needs.

90   For each pupil, examples of past and present work should be available in order to establish the range of work covered over time and to evaluate evidence of progress. Inspectors will find it helpful to have pupils' records available alongside their written work, including individual education plans or statements of special educational needs.

91   The evidence from analysing samples of work provides substantial confirmation of attainment and the breadth, depth and consolidation of learning. Other examples of pupils' work in classrooms, in exercise books or on display, help to establish how representative the sample is.

DISCUSSION WITH STAFF, THE 'APPROPRIATE AUTHORITY' AND OTHERS INVOLVED IN THE WORK OF THE SCHOOL

92   Headteachers and registered inspectors alike value a daily meeting to agree administrative details, discuss any matters of concern, clarify inspection issues and obtain further information. These meetings contribute a great deal to the smooth running of an inspection and the maintenance of good relationships by sharing emerging hypotheses, providing the opportunity for the school to offer further evidence, and preparing the way for some of the judgements made at the end of the inspection.

93   Discussions with the headteacher, representatives of the 'appropriate authority', staff with particular management responsibilities and class teachers provide important sources of evidence relating to roles and responsibilities, procedures and policies. They are essential to the professional dialogue between staff and inspectors, which contributes to the usefulness of inspection to schools. These discussions also help inspectors to establish the context for their observations.

94   Discussion with teachers, especially at the end of lessons or sessions, is desirable, but it may not always be possible to have more than a brief exchange. However, the work of teachers should be acknowledged and as many opportunities as possible found for professional dialogue. Such dialogue might involve clarifying the context of the lesson or session, and of future work, as well as providing a brief evaluation of the quality of work seen, where this is possible. In SHORT INSPECTIONS the discussion at the end of, or shortly after, the lesson should provide brief feedback whenever possible on the quality of the teaching observed and any significant strengths and weaknesses.

95   You should arrange to meet staff and representatives of the 'appropriate authority' to discuss their areas of responsibility at mutually convenient times. This is best arranged by negotiation before the inspection starts. Where possible you should indicate the points you wish to raise in the discussion, giving those concerned time to think about those issues. You should not offer a pro forma which teachers may feel under extra pressure to prepare for and complete. Take care that meetings do not make unreasonable demands on teachers' time, for instance their break times. To ensure efficient use of both teachers' and inspectors' time, you should plan and co-ordinate carefully the meetings with staff who have several responsibilities . Discussions with support staff, voluntary helpers and any visiting specialists, for example speech therapists, are also a valuable source of information and contribute to involving all staff in a FULL INSPECTION. It will not be possible to do this to the same extent on a SHORT INSPECTION.

THE PLACE OF DOCUMENTARY EVIDENCE

96 Schools should be judged primarily by their achievements, and on the effectiveness of their teaching, leadership and management in contributing to pupils' progress. Where a school is very effective, there is little need to trawl through all its procedural documents.

97 In the past, schools have spent an inordinate amount of time in preparing policies and revising curriculum plans or schemes, largely because of a forthcoming inspection. We wish to discourage this practice. Primary schools are required by regulations to have a number of procedures and policies in place; other policies are simply recommended or encouraged by the DfEE or other national organisations. The presence or absence of non-statutory policies or documents is not intrinsically material to the quality and standards of the school. For example, a school is unremarkable if it achieves good attendance in a situation where you would expect attendance to be good. Where attendance is surprisingly good or is unsatisfactory, then you should investigate either why the school has achieved such unusually high attendance or, conversely, the reasons for attendance being poor and what the school is doing or has done about it. In either of these cases, it is appropriate to look into the school's policy and procedures in respect of attendance, the way it handles absence, the dealings it has with parents over the question of attendance, and so on. A school should not be marked down simply for not having an attendance policy, unless the absence of such a policy, for example in a school with poor attendance, indicates a measure of complacency in dealing with the issue.

98 In all inspections, schools are asked to complete a school self-audit (*Form S3*). The school is not expected to undertake extensive audit activities in order to do this; it would normally be sufficiently well informed about what is required and how it meets those requirements. The form illustrates a range of areas in which statutory requirements apply to all or some schools. You should know what these requirements are.

99 In a SHORT INSPECTION, the small scale of the inspection means that only if a concern is raised during the inspection will the inspection team explore the school's compliance with the detail of statutory requirements. In a FULL INSPECTION, however, one or more inspectors from the team should follow up the school's compliance in a range of areas as part of, and relevant to, their responsibilities.

100 In a SHORT INSPECTION, inspectors should sample the planning which underpins some of the lessons they see, but should not *unless there is a significant concern* call for and inspect all the school's plans or schemes of work for different subjects. Nor should they ask for policy or operational documents unless they are material to the investigation of particular strengths and weaknesses.

101 In a FULL INSPECTION, inspectors should not require a school to produce voluminous documentation in advance of the inspection. They should look at the plans or schemes for the subjects they are inspecting as they exist in the school, either before or at an early stage in the inspection. The burden on schools of writing or photocopying must be kept to an *absolute* minimum, and schools should be reimbursed for any copying costs.

DISCUSSING YOUR FINDINGS WITH TEACHERS AND OTHER PARTIES

102 How well the messages given during feedback are received and acted upon depends much on the trust, respect and rapport established between you and the headteacher and staff during the inspection. The way you communicate findings is also important. You should therefore:

■ **gain teachers' acceptance;**

This includes talking with the teachers and other staff about their work as the inspection develops, showing sensitivity in your dealings with them and their pupils as evidence is collected, and interacting with the pupils as much as possible – though discreetly – during lesson observations.

■ **consider the effects of non-verbal as well as verbal messages during feedback and at other times;**

Eye contact and appropriate facial expression, posture, gesture, voice, pace and tone can all help to reduce anxiety, gain acceptance of inspection findings and encourage constructive professional dialogue. Oral messages and body language should always be compatible.

103 You should offer feedback to every teacher observed, and to teaching support assistants wherever you can. The objective is to help improve the teacher's effectiveness. You should try, whenever possible, to give firsthand feedback on the lessons you observe. The purpose is to let teachers know your perception of the quality of the lessons and responses of pupils: what went well; what was less successful; and what could be done more effectively. Feedback should therefore:

■ **identify the most important strengths and weaknesses in the teaching observed;**

You must be selective in what you say and not simply rehearse everything that you have seen. Illustrate general conclusions with specific and practical examples from the evidence you have. You should not strive to find weaknesses in teaching that has none.

■ **provide clear reasons for what you judged to be successful or otherwise;**

Strengths and weaknesses should always be linked to their effects on pupils' learning, and must be attributed to the teaching approaches used rather than the teacher.

■ **ensure that points for development are identified.**

Where the teaching is less than satisfactory, you should diagnose precisely what is not working and spell out what is needed to bring about improvement. But it is equally important to identify how satisfactory and good teaching can be improved. You should, of course, acknowledge very good teaching and the features that make it so, but even here it is helpful if more subtle improvements can be identified.

FEEDBACK ON LESSONS

104   Where teaching is effective, feedback can usually be managed successfully after lessons – either at the end of the lesson if this is possible, or at a later time during the day if this is more convenient. Where there are concerns, you may need time to reflect upon what you have seen and, more particularly, upon how you might best discuss your findings with the teacher concerned. It is helpful to see more than one lesson before feeding back about unsatisfactory teaching, to gauge whether weaknesses are sustained.

105   In a SHORT INSPECTION, the team is unlikely to be able to see a sufficient sample of the work of all teachers to give a view of the overall quality of their teaching. Some will not be seen teaching; others may only be visited for a single lesson. In very effective schools, one expects to see few, if any, weaknesses in the teaching. You are not required to provide summary feedback to teachers towards or at the end of the inspection but you should give whatever feedback you can as you go along. In SHORT INSPECTIONS, teachers will not be given a profile of the judgements on their teaching.

106   In a FULL INSPECTION, you should offer teachers summary feedback on the teaching that has been observed. Towards the end of the inspection, strengths and weaknesses in what has been seen can be pulled together. A number of inspectors may see a substantial sample of the work of every teacher. So summary feedback to an individual at the end of the inspection needs to be carefully co-ordinated to ensure that the inspector responsible for the feedback is well informed. Wherever possible, the inspector who is assigned to give feedback to a particular teacher should be the one who is best placed, by virtue of expertise or firsthand evidence collected, to make the greatest contribution to the professional development of that teacher. At the end of the inspection, each teacher is given a written record of the inspectors' judgements of their teaching, with a copy to the headteacher.

107   The requirement for individual performance feedback applies to:

- full-time and part-time teachers;

- supply teachers, except those working for less than five days in the school;

- teachers funded under Ethnic Minorities Achievement Grant (EMAG) and other grants for specific purposes;

- others, such as qualified support teachers, where they are responsible for classes or groups of children or the focus of evaluation of teaching has been on their work.

108   The requirement to provide individual performance feedback does not apply to the following staff and helpers, although you should offer it where possible. These staff are not given the written profile of judgements about their teaching, where their work was the focus of observation. However, you should include as many of these people as possible in ongoing dialogue. Their recorded work will be collated under a composite heading OTHER CONTRIBUTIONS TO TEACHING in the profile given to the headteacher. The profile of judgements is not given to:

- trainee teachers;

- nursery and other classroom assistants;

- special needs support assistants;

- non-teaching support assistants;

- artists and writers in residence;

- instructors and coaches;

- visitors and other voluntary helpers.

FEEDBACK TO CO-ORDINATORS

109   Feedback to those with management responsibility for subjects or key aspects of the school's work is essential. Usually there is 'drip-feeding' of evaluations and sharing of hypotheses during the inspection, and summary feedback at the end of the week. There should be no major surprises at the end of the inspection. The summary feedback should:

- present the significant inspection findings supported by sufficient evidence so that the reasons for judgements are understood;

- provide an opportunity to clarify the findings;

- explore areas of disagreement;

- examine priorities for action;

- give the co-ordinator a clear basis on which to start planning for improvement.

110   In a SHORT INSPECTION, you are unlikely to see a large enough sample of work to come to unequivocal views of quality and standards in all the subjects of the curriculum. In these circumstances, and taking account of the brevity of the inspection, you are not required to offer feedback to subject co-ordinators at the end of the inspection. It is enough to do what you can as you go along.

111   In a FULL INSPECTION, feedback should be given to as many co-ordinators as possible, depending on how much work of each subject it has been possible to see. At a minimum, feedback should be given to the co-ordinators of the core subjects of English, mathematics, science, information technology and, where relevant, religious education. It should give them a clear picture of the inspection findings in their subject. In particular, it should rehearse the significant evidence and judgements about:

- standards in the subject;

- the quality of teaching and learning in the subject;

- improvement since the last inspection;

- areas identified as particular strengths and weaknesses;

- issues identified by inspection as priorities for improving the school.

AFTER THE INSPECTION

THE FINAL TEAM MEETING

112   The main purpose of this team meeting is to arrive at accurate and thoroughly secure corporate judgements about the school, recording these in the *Record of Corporate Judgements*. You, as the registered inspector, need to manage this meeting so that the hypthoses tested out during the inspection are discussed and conclusions reached. You need to bring judgements together so that the culmination of the meeting is the team's overall view of the effectiveness of the school. The strengths and weaknesses recorded in WHAT THE SCHOOL DOES WELL and WHAT COULD BE IMPROVED also need to be specifically agreed by the team.

113   Therefore, all inspectors need to have reflected on their evidence, to have reached their own views, and to be prepared to contribute these at the meeting. This means the meeting must not take place immediately after the inspection finishes. If the inspection finishes at lunchtime, you will need time to complete your *Inspection Notebook* in a FULL INSPECTION, or to gather your thoughts together in a SHORT INSPECTION before a meeting later in the afternoon. If the inspection finishes at the end of the school day, the final team meeting must not be held that day.

114   The meeting must be structured to achieve the goals set out above. In particular, the following areas must be included:

■ discussions leading to the completion of the *Record of Corporate Judgements*;

■ agreement about the contents of the summary of the inspection report;

■ consideration, as a team, whether the school is in need of special measures, has serious weaknesses or is underachieving.

115   We expect that all inspectors will attend this team meeting. We recognise that there will be exceptional circumstances where this is not possible. If that is the case, the inspector concerned must provide the registered inspector with his/her completed *Inspection Notebook* (except the draft text for the report) and any additional points that need to be brought to the attention of other inspectors.

FEEDBACK TO THE HEADTEACHER AND SENIOR STAFF

116   Your feedback should give senior management an early but firm basis on which to start planning in response to the inspection's findings. In particular, the feedback to senior management should rehearse the significant evidence and judgements about:

■ the school's outcomes, particularly standards achieved by pupils;

■ the factors which most account for what is achieved, particularly the strengths and weaknesses in teaching in the school;

■ the effectiveness of work done by managers and co-ordinators;

■ the issues identified by inspection as priorities for improving the school.

117   The staff attending the meeting should have the opportunity to clarify any of these findings, ask for further examples of evidence on which particular judgements about the school are based, and explore with inspectors the priorities for action.

118   The feedback to the headteacher and invited staff must be after the inspection has finished. It must not be on the last day of the inspection or even the day after. As the registered inspector, you must leave sufficient time to reflect on the evidence and corporate judgements in order to prepare properly.

119   The headteacher can invite whom he or she wishes to the feedback meeting, but it is usually for the senior management team only. No one other than the staff of the school should normally attend. There may be exceptional circumstances when the presence of an LEA officer as an observer is justified, for example:

   ■ if the school has a temporary headteacher pending a permanent appointment;

   ■ if a two-teacher school is staffed only by the headteacher and his or her spouse or partner;

   ■ if the headteacher is judged likely to find the inspection findings distressing.

120   In such exceptional circumstances, the school can invite the officer only with the consent of the registered inspector.

121   The formal feedback should not be confused with the interim feedback offered to headteachers towards the end of an inspection by many registered inspectors. This is helpful to the school in relieving uncertainties and stress.

FEEDBACK TO THE 'APPROPRIATE AUTHORITY'

122   The success of the feedback to the 'appropriate authority', usually the governing body, hinges on how effectively inspectors communicate the main inspection findings clearly and frankly to a mixed audience, many of whom are well-informed but not professional teachers or educators. The same general principles apply to giving feedback to the governing body as to the senior management team, but the presentation to the governing body should have much less detail. The presentation should include a careful explanation of specific matters which should be included in the post-inspection plan. This is to ensure that the governing body is clear at an early stage about what the school should do to improve. It will often help to use visual aids to summarise the main points of the presentation.

123   The governing body for an LEA-maintained school may, if it wishes, invite an LEA officer (or diocesan education officer or similar religious adviser in the case of schools with a religious character) to be present as an observer at the oral feedback to the governing body. In most cases you will wish to include these observers in the dialogue. However, as the registered inspector, you may need to remind observers of their role if they become too assertive.

SOME GENERAL POINTS ABOUT FEEDBACK

124   Formal, feedback meetings must take place before the inspection report is finished and as soon as is practicable after the inspection. The content of the oral feedback is confidential and the findings of the inspection should not be released, particularly to parents and the press, until after the 'appropriate authority' has received the report. You may wish to remind those attending these meetings of their confidentiality.

125   The quality of the feedback is an important factor in influencing how the school responds to the inspection findings, and particularly in drawing up its post-inspection action plan for improvement. Effective feedback:

- is well structured, clear, succinct and unrushed;

- makes use of appropriate visual aids to help communicate the inspection findings, especially to governing bodies;

- places greater emphasis on what the school does well and what could be improved, and why, but also covers the relevant reporting requirements in the *Evaluation Schedule*;

- presents a balanced and rounded picture of the school;

- gives well-chosen examples or observations that show you know the school;

- allows opportunities for discussion and clarification of the inspection findings;

- avoids giving detailed advice to the school about how to tackle the improvements that are needed.

126   It is expected that all oral reporting will proceed smoothly and professionally and that feedback will be of value to staff and governors alike. If, however, the behaviour of those at a feedback meeting makes it impossible to proceed with a sensible professional dialogue, you as the registered inspector have the right to confine the feedback simply to the main findings of the inspection and the key issues for action. In extreme cases, you have the right not to proceed with the oral report.

127   The use of tape recorders by headteachers, governing bodies and individual teachers at feedback meetings is entirely at the discretion of the registered inspector. It is reasonable for you not to proceed with a feedback meeting if there is any insistence on their use against your will. OFSTED has no objection to the tape recording of feedback meetings if the registered inspector agrees.

THE REPORT AND THE SUMMARY OF THE REPORT

STANDARDS OF REPORTING

128 The inspection report must be a carefully considered, clearly written and well-checked document of high quality. It must relay the inspection findings as unequivocal judgements in clear, straightforward language so that:

- parents, governors, the staff of the school and other readers get a clear picture of the quality and standards of the school, an understanding of its strengths and weaknesses, and insights into why the school achieves as it does;

- the school has a good basis for subsequent action to improve standards and the quality of education.

129 The report should reflect the individual school. It is unique to the school and must, on no account, duplicate in whole or in part the text of earlier reports, however similar the school. The report must follow the structure set out in the *Evaluation Schedule* but its content, wording and style should not be written to any pre-determined formula. Key judgements must be absolutely clear, and consistent with the oral feedback given to the school and governors. Reasons for judgements should be given to enable readers to understand why the inspection team has arrived at its views. While judgements should be based on the criteria set out in the *Evaluation Schedule*, the report should focus on strengths and areas where improvement is needed. It is not necessary to allude to each and every criterion in the schedule, nor to quote the criteria parrot-fashion.

130 It is essential that the report provides clear interpretations of any performance data and presents the inspection team's judgements about the educational standards achieved by pupils at the school. Overall judgements should be illustrated by reference to the strengths and weaknesses in the areas of learning or different subjects or courses of the curriculum, with particular emphasis placed on the core subjects of English, mathematics, science, information technology and, where inspected, religious education.

131 The report must explain any apparent inconsistencies, for example where teaching is generally good but achievement is poor.

132 When reporting on the quality of education provided, inspectors must focus, in particular, on the quality of teaching and learning. Other aspects of provision are important only for their effect on the quality of teaching and learning and the educational standards achieved. Where those other aspects of provision are unexceptional, further justification is usually unnecessary. Where there are particular strengths and weaknesses, though, amplification is needed in order to explain why, for example, mathematics teaching is 'outstanding' or leadership is 'weak'.

133 The **summary report** and the section of the report on WHAT SHOULD THE SCHOOL DO TO IMPROVE FURTHER? are particularly important. The summary is the report for parents and needs particularly careful drafting to communicate effectively with a wide readership. It must draw out the key judgements about the school and leave it without any doubt about the strengths and weaknesses of the school. The contents of the summary, particularly the sections on WHAT THE SCHOOL DOES WELL and WHAT COULD BE IMPROVED, must be consistent with the rest of the report.

134   The report, and its summary, should therefore:

- be clear to all its readers, governors, parents, professionals and the public at large;

- concentrate on evaluating rather than describing what is seen;

- focus on the educational standards achieved and the factors which impact on standards and quality;

- use everyday language, not educational jargon, and be grammatically correct;

- be specific in its judgements;

- use sub-headings, bullet points and other devices where they help to make the messages clear;

- use telling examples drawn from the evidence base to make generalisations understandable and to illustrate what is meant by 'good' or 'poor';

- employ words and phrases that enliven the report and convey the individual character of the school.

135   Readers of the summary report will not necessarily read the full report. The summary report must, therefore, be capable of standing alone as a fair and balanced picture of the school, and the steps needed to improve it.

136   The summary report must include the elements specified in the *Evaluation Schedule*. In addition, the summary report must include the standard text specified in the report template issued to inspectors.

137   The report and summary of the report must be produced within six calendar weeks from the end of the inspection and forwarded without delay to the 'appropriate authority', HMCI and persons specified in sections 16 and 20 of the 1996 Act. The 'appropriate authority' must previously have had five working days to comment on the draft version of the report.

STRUCTURE OF REPORTS

138   The structure is shown schematically on page 147. All inspection reports include the summary of the report (Part A), the commentary (Part B) and a data section (Part C). **Reports of** FULL **INSPECTIONS also include a subject section (Part D). Reports of** SHORT **and** FULL **INSPECTIONS differ markedly in the structure of the commentary.**

139   In SHORT INSPECTIONS, the commentary is based on the two sections of the summary entitled WHAT THE SCHOOL DOES WELL and WHAT COULD BE IMPROVED. Each of the strengths and weaknesses listed in these two sections of the summary becomes a sub-heading of the commentary. For example, if the first item in WHAT THE SCHOOL DOES WELL is: 'Pupils' writing and mathematics are excellent', then this finding becomes the first sub-heading for the commentary. The commentary of short reports, therefore, does not follow the headings provided by the *Evaluation Schedule*.

140   In FULL INSPECTIONS, the commentary of the report follows the structure set out in the *Evaluation Schedule*.

PRESENTATION OF THE PRE-PUBLICATION REPORT TO THE SCHOOL

141 The school has five working days in which to consider the final, pre-publication draft of the inspection report to check the factual accuracy of its content. *The registered inspector must ensure that the report shown to the school is his or her intended final report and is of publication quality. By this stage it must have taken account of comments made by any editorial reader hired by the contractor.* Showing this report to the school is not meant to be an opportunity to negotiate judgements. The report should contain no surprises. It should reflect precisely the judgements conveyed during oral feedback to the senior managers and the 'appropriate authority'.

REPORTING REQUIREMENTS

REPORT

SUMMARY

+

COMMENTARY

THIS IS PART A OF THE REPORT

- Information about the school
- How good the school is

followed by a list of the main strengths of the school and any weaknesses under the headings:

- What the school does well
- What could be improved

If the school is judged to be underachieving, or is identified as having serious weaknesses or requiring special measures, this should be stated.

- How the school has improved since its last inspection
- Standards
- Pupils' attitudes and values
- Teaching and learning
- Other aspects of the school
- How well is the school led and managed?
- Parents' and carers' views of the school

SHORT INSPECTION

FULL INSPECTION

THIS IS PART B OF THE REPORT

A commentary on each of the issues listed in:

- What the school does well

  and
- What could be improved

  followed by sections on:
- What should the school do to improve further?
- Other specified features (if any)

THIS IS PART C OF THE REPORT

Data tables

Summary of responses to parents' questionnaire

THIS IS PART B OF THE REPORT

- How high are the standards?

  The school's results and pupils' achievements

  Pupils' attitudes, values and personal development
- How well are pupils taught?
- How good are the curricular and other opportunities offered to pupils?
- How well does the school care for its pupils?
- How well does the school work in partnership with parents?
- How well is the school led and managed?
- What should the school do to improve further?
- Other specified features (if any)

THIS IS PART C OF THE REPORT

Data tables

Summary of responses to parents' questionnaire

THIS IS PART D OF THE REPORT

- The standards and quality of teaching in areas of the curriculum and subjects

The summary report must include:

- all statutory reporting requirements;
- required judgements about each of the ☐ headings for sections 1–9 of the *Evaluation Schedule* and, in FULL INSPECTIONS, a summary of the strengths and weaknesses from section 10 of the *Schedule*.

PART 3

USING THE *HANDBOOK* FOR SCHOOL SELF-EVALUATION

SELF-EVALUATION

The school that knows and understands itself is well on the way to solving any problems it has. The school that is ignorant of its weaknesses, or will not, or cannot, face up to them is not well managed. Self-evaluation provides the key to improvement. The ability to generate a commitment among staff to appraise their own work critically, and that of others, is a key test of how well a school is managed.

Effective change and self-evaluation are characterised by openness and consultation and are a regular part of the good school's working life in which everyone is encouraged to participate. Self-evaluation complements inspection with a constant process of identifying priorities for improvement, monitoring provision and evaluating outcomes.

Both inspection and internal evaluation are concerned with providing an accurate appraisal of the quality and standards of the school and diagnosing what needs to be done to improve them. Inspectors have a duty to report, via the governing body, to parents. Schools are encouraged to do the same with their self-evaluation findings.

It is advantageous to base school self-evaluation on the same criteria as those used in all schools by inspectors. A common language has developed about the work of schools, expressed through the criteria. Teachers and governors know that the criteria reflect things that matter.

The guidance on inspection published for inspectors in the first revision of the OFSTED *Handbooks*[2] is accepted by headteachers as a sound basis for evaluation, defining a useful range of criteria to assess the quality and impact of what schools provide for pupils. *School Evaluation Matters*[3] exemplifies and illustrates the work of many schools for whom monitoring and evaluation are central to improvement. *Making the Most of Inspection*[4] helps schools to see external inspection as one aspect of evaluation, which can be actively used to promote improvement.

Self-evaluation is not about being an inspector. By using this guidance you should be able to undertake an annual analysis of the standards and the effectiveness of your actions.

There are four questions that are at the heart of evaluating everything you do:

■ **Are all the pupils in my school learning as much as they are capable of learning?**

■ **What can I do to find out?**

■ **When I answer this question how do I know I am right?**

■ **What do I do about it when I have the answer?**

---

[2] The OFSTED *Handbooks: Guidance on the Inspection of Nursery, Primary, Secondary and Special Schools*, HMSO 1995.

[3] OFSTED Publications Centre 1998.

[4] OFSTED Publications Centre 1998.

To ensure that self-evaluation has the maximum impact on standards:

- take an objective look at pupils' achievements and pinpoint areas of underachievement;

- account for outcomes in your school by identifying strengths and weaknesses in teaching, before looking at what else you provide to support learning;

- use this information to devise the School Improvement (Development) Plan, which is at its best when seen simply as a means to raise standards.

WHAT POINT HAVE YOU REACHED?

In 1997–98 one in three of all schools was judged to be good, or very good, at monitoring and evaluating the quality of its work, and a further one in three was judged to be satisfactory. The remaining one-third were unsatisfactory. Primary schools were generally slightly better at this than secondary schools. Although these proportions show an improvement since the beginning of the OFSTED inspection cycle, there is still much work to be done.[5]

Primary and nursery schools vary in their management of evaluation. For example, one primary school:

> monitors performance at pupil and class level; uses value-added indicators in reading and mathematics; places a clear responsibility on co-ordinators of the core subjects to monitor and evaluate work in those subjects across the school and provides time for them to do it; appraises the work of each teacher annually; and surveys parents about their perceptions of the school.

In another primary school, the headteacher, in agreement with the staff, used their recent training in teaching numeracy as the basis for their self-evaluation (*see Example 1 on page 157*).

School self-evaluation is about diagnosis and change in the way people work, and this is particularly so for teaching and its impact. But it must carry a 'health warning'. It can be a mistake to 'do a self-evaluation' of the whole school, treating it as one event like 'having an inspection'. It is far better that inspection complements a process of identifying and nibbling away at priorities through regular monitoring and evaluation.

- **If you have not introduced a strategy for monitoring and evaluating** the work of your school, your area of responsibility, or your own work in the classroom, you will find the *Handbook* particularly helpful.

- **If some monitoring and evaluation is in place**, this guidance will enable you to assess how effectively you undertake it.

- **If you feel there is already 'continuous evaluation'**, you will be able to check whether such blanket coverage is concealing some prime suspects for investigation.

- **If you feel there is little we can tell you about self-evaluation**, then we should be pleased if you would tell us more about what you do.

Wherever you are up to, *Form S4* (on the CD-ROM attached to this *Handbook*) is about self-evaluation. It is for the inspection team, but we believe that many headteachers and governors will find *Form S4* a useful basis for the regular evaluation of the progress their school is making, across all its work, whether or not it is being inspected.

---

[5] Data taken from *Primary Education 1994–98*, HMSO 1999; and *Secondary Education 1993–97*, HMSO 1998.

WHERE DO YOU BEGIN?

There are several possible starting points. They may include:

- **areas identified by senior management or the governing body as needing improvement;**

  which may have arisen as a result of monitoring performance, evidence of problems, a survey of parents or staff, or for other reasons;

- **interest by one or more particular staff;**

  in which case they should be helped and encouraged, and their work used as a pilot for wider adoption;

- **a known area of strength or weakness in the school;**

  which can then be evaluated and the reasons for success or lack of it diagnosed;

- **an inspection report;**

  in which issues are identified that need to be investigated further as a basis for action.

Two of the most systematic spurs to self-evaluation are the appraisal of teachers, and the monitoring and analysis of performance. Inspectors start from the latter point, as illustrated in Part 2 of this *Handbook*. Monitoring and analysing performance have the advantage of illuminating where to focus your evaluative effort. Appraisal, on the other hand, applies to all and is a major undertaking.

EVALUATING STANDARDS

Start with monitoring standards and related matters. Strong internal reviews look first at key measurable outcomes. Your monitoring of measurable outcomes, such as standards, should result in evaluation that examines the quality and impact of what you provide. For instance, use:

- baseline data of attainment on entry;

- analysis of test results and teacher assessments;

- a study of ethnicity and gender balances in your results;

- test analysis;

- monitoring to know how many pupils reach their performance targets;

- standards in the school measured against other schools;

- value-added information;

- an analysis of pupils' work by pupil type and across Key Stages;

- an analysis of attendance and punctuality patterns;

- interviews with staff about their classes;

- a review of governors' attitudes to standards in your school;

- questions to parents about what they think of what your school does.

You will want to: analyse standards on entry; predict the maximum possible gains in knowledge, understanding and skills for pupils and set appropriate goals; determine how these can best be achieved; analyse performance at the end of each year and Key Stage; record the progress made by pupils, and decide where, if anywhere, improvements are needed.

Your **Performance and Assessment Report (PANDA)** provides data to help answer the question: **How high are standards?** Your school is likely to have other data available, such as the results of standardised tests used for diagnostic purposes, baseline assessments, or value-added data. The guidance in section 2 of Part 1 of this *Handbook* will help steer you through the analytical process needed in order to form an objective view of the standards reached by your pupils, and whether or not pupils achieve as much as they should.

The data should give you a good picture of trends over time. It also shows relative achievements in the core subjects. Analysis of the data should prompt questions such as: *Why are so few pupils achieving level 5 in mathematics? Why is writing apparently so much weaker than reading? Why are results not better midway through Key Stage 2?*

The analysis of data, therefore, can provide an immediate focus for self-evaluation. In the subjects that are not tested or formally assessed in primary schools, other information about quality is needed in the absence of test and assessment data. You may start, for example, by looking carefully at the standard of work done or recorded by pupils to get a first indication of where strengths and weaknesses lie. Sometimes in a primary school, one teacher may be unusually effective or ineffective in much of the work they do with their class. In the case of such weakness, evaluation of teaching becomes an appraisal of competence: a different issue.

If you are a headteacher of a nursery school you are unlikely to have the same kind of performance data. Your evaluation of standards will want to focus on the progress the children have made from the time they came to you. You may wish to use your entry profiles, completed when children started at the nursery, as well as any information from parents about their child.

EVALUATING TEACHING

The monitoring, evaluation and support of teaching are central to school effectiveness and improvement. Systematic monitoring of teaching through classroom observation is relatively rare. As a result, in many schools senior staff lack the knowledge they need if they are to help raise standards. The observation and evaluation of teaching and learning should be based on clear and understood criteria. Section 3 of Part 1 of this *Handbook* – HOW WELL ARE PUPILS TAUGHT? – gives national criteria for judging teaching and learning, together with guidance on their application.

The section entitled *Making Judgements* states clearly the characteristics of very good teaching and unsatisfactory teaching. You may initially want to focus on one subject or aspect of teaching.

You will see that the overriding consideration for evaluating the quality of teaching is how well pupils learn. This is judged not only by assessing their knowledge, understanding and skills, but by looking at the extent of their engagement in the lesson, the pace of their work and the demands made on them. If these are good, decide what are the features of teaching which have this effect. If the converse is true, you need to diagnose what is not working well enough and consider what could be done to improve matters. Evaluation and setting an agenda for development are starting points, but are of limited value unless the monitoring of classroom teaching is systematic; carried out to agreed criteria; and the outcomes discussed with teachers.

The section on *Guidance on using the Evaluation Schedule* helps you to know what to look for in your lesson observations. You can use the *Evaluation Forms* on the CD-ROM to record the information. Before the observation ensure that teachers know what your focus will be. Try to make sure that it arises from the monitoring you have done of standards. During lesson observations, record what teachers do well and less well, always judge their work by the impact it has on pupils' learning. Note how pupils respond during the lesson, watch how their attitudes to learning and their behaviour influence the standards they reach. Try to record how much learning has taken place during your observation, measured by talking with pupils, examining their work and looking back through their work to see where they have come from, and gauge their progress.

As you conclude an observation decide how effective the lesson was overall, which parts worked best and which – if any – did not work so well. Did all pupils in the class gain from the demands made of them? Did all the teaching techniques and elements of the lesson contribute well to the intended outcomes? Where were the strengths and weaknesses? What could be done more effectively in future?

FEEDING BACK AFTER OBSERVING LESSONS, AND ONGOING SUPPORT

It is essential to have an agreed format for feeding back your considered evaluation of teaching. Schools may use different ways of doing this. Some do it collectively, with the group of staff involved, others individually. The guidance provided for inspectors in Part 2 of this *Handbook*, on giving feedback, may be helpful to you.

Evaluation should lead to personal or team agendas for becoming more effective. These should include targets for improvement, against which progress may be monitored through regular structured follow-up observations to see if the targets have been realised. It is important that management supports these agendas in all possible ways, which may include professional development, the acquisition of resources and the opportunity to visit teachers in other classes or schools.

PERFORMANCE MANAGEMENT AND LEADING IMPROVEMENT

If you are a headteacher or governor, performance management is now an integral part of your work. The 1999 *School Teachers' Pay and Conditions Document*[6] stipulates that headteachers' professional duties include:

> *evaluating the standards of teaching and learning in the school, and ensuring that proper standards of professional performance are established and maintained.*

Many would argue that all staff with management responsibilities have similar obligations. Performance is rightly associated with the standards achieved and the quality of learning. Performance management policies will centre on the assessment of teaching, and analysis of pupils' progress and learning, to guide the setting of targets for improvement and development over the next year. The governing body has responsibility for appraising the performance of the headteacher, setting appropriate targets for the headteacher and deciding on performance-related pay for the headteacher and staff.

---

[6] *Schoolteachers' Pay and Conditions Document 1999*, paragraph 43.7.

Performance management is most effective where there is:

■ strong, well-motivated and clear-sighted leadership;

■ rigorous analysis of standards;

■ continuous monitoring and evaluation of teaching and learning;

■ wholehearted commitment from staff to the school and to self-improvement;

■ a set of easily understood objectives and reasonable but challenging targets at all levels;

■ plenty of support for development and improvement;

■ good management of resources, including financial incentives and rewards that maximise performance.

The impact of your management and leadership and of those who support you in running the school will dictate how governors, staff, pupils and parents see the quality of your performance as the headteacher. The *Evaluation Schedule* section 7, HOW WELL IS THE SCHOOL LED AND MANAGED?, will help you to review and improve your own performance and that of any senior colleagues you may have. Remember that you may not be the best person to lead such an evaluation. Involve teachers new to the school, parents, governors and staff. Some schools also involve pupils in school evaluation. The section headed *Making Judgements* makes clear the vital features of good leaders and managers, and the section on leadership and management will help you to find ways of measuring the impact of what you and your colleagues do, and how it benefits pupils.

As the headteacher, you are strongly influential in providing a culture in which the cycle of self-evaluation and development is valued, understood, published and communicated. It is crucially important that you assure its effectiveness and ensure that everyone in the school is involved in, and committed to, their own learning as part of maximising pupils' achievements. Thus to be at your best you, your staff and governors should be reflective and analytical when weighing up the value, or effectiveness, of what you provide.

USING INSPECTION TO COMPLEMENT SELF-EVALUATION

Inspection, well used, complements good self-evaluation. During an inspection there will be a number of opportunities for you and your staff to: test your perceptions of the school against those of impartial, external evaluators; receive feedback; and discuss the quality and standards being achieved. Making the most of these opportunities, and the discussions and professional debates during the more formal feedback meetings, will provide additional valuable information to add to your own evaluation of your school. Together with the key issues, all these points will help you and your governors to prepare an action plan and direct your school improvement planning.

As with the outcomes of your self-evaluation activities, use inspection to celebrate success. It is essential to recognise where the school is doing well, and to compliment those involved, as well as to tackle matters that need to be improved. It is particularly important to be positive and forward-looking after the inspection is over and the report has arrived, or after any phase of intensive evaluation, in order to combat the sense of anticlimax which can prevail, even with the most resounding endorsement of the school.

SCHOOL SELF-EVALUATION IN A NUTSHELL

Start now

Accept that we can all improve

Place the raising of standards at the heart of all your planning

Measure standards

Compare yourself with others

Regularly observe each other teaching to a set of agreed and rigorous criteria

Evaluate the effect that teaching has on learning

Be completely open in feeding back what you find

Think, discuss and consult

Set targets for everyone's improvement

Ensure that action is supported, monitored and reviewed

Never stop evaluating

Example 1

Making evaluation manageable: a specific focus on mathematics teaching in a primary school

The headteacher and staff of a four-teacher school had just completed in-service work on the teaching of numeracy. The headteacher wanted to monitor the impact of the training. In agreement with staff she decided to focus on one aspect of mathematics lessons at a time.

The first question the school sought to answer was:

Do we make the best use of the end part (plenary) of our mathematics lessons?

The school used:

- *the criteria for judging the quality of teaching;*

- *prompts from the* Framework for Teaching Mathematics *to guide the analysis of pupils' responses;*

- Evidence Forms *to record lesson observations.*

Evidence came from:

- *teachers' plans;*

- *discussions with pupils;*

- *observations of parts of lessons;*

- *discussions with teachers.*

How and when the evidence was gathered:

- *by the headteacher who noted down learning objectives from her own and her colleagues' planning;*

- *using fifteen minutes of her administration day for three successive weeks, she observed the mathematics plenaries across the school;*

- *the numeracy consultant for the LEA taught the class of the mathematics co-ordinator so that she could observe her colleagues', including the headteacher's, plenaries;*

- *the co-ordinator met with the pupils she was tracking (a low-attainer, a high-attainer and an average-attainer from each year group) to discuss what they had learned in their mathematics lesson;*

- *those pupils from Key Stage 2 were also asked to reflect on the ways the plenary helped them to learn;*

- *evidence on the strengths and weaknesses of plenaries was gathered from a staff meeting.*

(continued overleaf)

(Example continued)

The evidence was analysed:

- *by the headteacher and co-ordinator, using evidence from their Evidence Forms, to examine the ways in which plenaries were used to reinforce learning objectives;*

- *they noted the most and least effective aspects of teaching and cross-referenced this information with notes from discussions with pupils and teachers.*

The evidence told them:

- *that in two cases, plenaries were not directly linked to the learning objectives;*

- *time was not well managed in one class and the plenary was rushed;*

- *in the co-ordinator's class, the plenary was very effective;*

- *questions were often closed giving pupils little scope to show their learning.*

Staff acknowledged that they found it difficult to structure open questions to test particular aspects of learning.

In general, the pupils enjoyed talking about what they had learned but felt that some groups had more time to explain their work than others. For pupils from one class the plenary was usually very short and sometimes did not happen at all.

Improvements proposed to staff:

- *sharpen the focus of plenaries;*

- *co-ordinator to plan in-service on formulating open questions;*

- *joint planning to link learning objectives to the plenary;*

- *headteacher to work with member of staff to improve management of time.*

Monitoring implications:

- *agree targets for measuring improvement;*

- *monitor further lessons to ensure that planning is implemented;*

- *set date to meet with pupils to test out their views of the changes implemented;*

- *set date with the numeracy consultant to provide release time for the co-ordinator;*

- *set date and time to collate information from co-ordinator, governor and pupils;*

- *work with the mathematics co-ordinator to review progress;*

- *evaluate mathematics lessons as a whole.*

PART 4

ANNEXES

ANNEX 1

JUDGING BEST VALUE PRINCIPLES AND FINANCIAL MANAGEMENT IN SCHOOLS

There is a statutory duty on local authorities (in general, not just LEAs) to obtain best value by securing economic, efficient and effective services. The best value framework, within which local authorities are required to respond to local needs and make decisions locally, primarily focuses on the balance between cost and quality in striving continuously to improve services.

The best value approach does not apply statutorily to governing bodies in their use of delegated and devolved budgets. However, governing bodies are required to set targets to raise standards, are expected to provide a good-quality public service, and spend public money wisely. Schools are accountable for balancing *costs* (in terms of economy and efficiency) and *effectiveness* (in terms of their performance and the quality of what they provide) as required by the best value framework. To achieve this schools need to demonstrate that they apply best value principles in arriving at decisions about all their activities, especially how the financial resources delegated to them are managed.

Your task on inspection is, in light of all the available evidence, to evaluate and report on how effectively the school applies best value principles in its management and use of resources.

INSPECTION AND THE BEST VALUE FRAMEWORK

Inspecting the use of the best value framework fits easily within the overall inspection process. Both require attention to be given to evaluating the school's performance and its management and planning processes. One sign of effective planning is, for example, a challenging and appropriately costed school development plan.

The best value framework covers four principles (summarised as the four 'Cs'), each of which is linked to specific requirements in the *Evaluation Schedule*:

- Compare;

- Challenge;

- Consult;

- Compete.

The following are examples of questions you may wish to use, grouped under the headings related to the four principles.

COMPARE: Comparison of performance against that of all schools and similar schools is readily possible for primary schools. *PANDA reports* and other data provide suitable benchmarks and other indicators to enable the school to monitor its performance, measure it against others and set targets. Find out the extent to which the school asks itself, and answers, such questions as:

■ *What is the quality of education provided by similar schools?*

■ *How do our standards compare with theirs?*

■ *Are we a relatively high performer?*

■ *Do we cost more or less than others?*

■ *Why?*

Guidance on evaluating value for money appears in Part 1 of this *Handbook*.

CHALLENGE: This is about whether the school challenges itself about the services it provides. Does the school take steps, for example, to find out whether what it provides is what is needed, within the discretion allowed in the statutory framework for the curriculum and outside the statutory minimum? Although, for primary schools, the National Curriculum is not negotiable, other aspects of provision are. Does the introduction of primary French, a 'silent reading' period for every class, or a part-time play group on the school premises, for example, fulfil the conditions of best value? Find out the extent to which the school asks itself such questions as:

■ *Why are we doing this?*

■ *Is it what people want?*

■ *What is the evidence about level of need?*

■ *Could someone else do it differently, or better?*

CONSULT: This is about being clear what the school community wants. When considering major changes or spending decisions, involving the curriculum provided or other major developments, does the school seek the views of those most concerned, and how does it respond to those views? This means asking or getting feedback from staff, parents, pupils and others on:

■ *what they want the school to do;*

■ *what they think of proposed changes or major expenditure;*

■ *whether they are happy with, or at, the school;*

■ *what is in their best interests.*

Did the school consult parents, for example, when drawing up a post-inspection action plan? or when changing the balance of the curriculum? Or does it just announce such matters? Increasingly, schools use questionnaires to survey parents; many also periodically seek the views of pupils. Some primary schools have a pupils' council. Indeed some involve young pupils to the extent of producing a version of the summary inspection report specially written for pupils.

COMPETE: Competition is concerned both with whether the school is doing anything which could be better provided by someone else, and with the strategic use of resources and getting best value for expenditure. Does the school have proper financial administration procedures, including competitive tendering for significant expenditure? Examples might include supply and part-time staff, in-service training, expenditure on equipment and maintenance contracts. Is purchasing on a fair and open basis or through personal connection, or is one supplier used regardless of price? The school should be asking questions like:

- *Are we providing the service at the right price?*

- *Could we or others provide it at a better price?*

- *What do the users of this service want?*

- *What is in the best interest of pupils and parents?*

- *How does the school ensure it receives the most economic, efficient and effective service from those who provide services to pupils and staff?*

You will need to determine whether the school manages its decision-making and assesses the impact on standards of its spending and other decisions in ways that reflect the best value framework. You will need to find out how it balances *costs* (in terms of economy and efficiency) and *effectiveness* (in terms of the performance of the school and the quality of what it provides). This has implications for how you gather and test the evidence from the whole of the inspection, for example your analysis of performance in section 2 and your evaluation of school provision in sections 3 and 4 of the *Evaluation Schedule*.

It is not, however, for inspectors to judge whether best value is being positively achieved; such a judgement is a matter for local accountability. What is required of inspectors is to make information available to parents and other local people about whether the school is applying the best value principle effectively and for them to come to a view about whether best value is being achieved.

Some schools will be more familiar with the principles of best value than others, although some of the elements, such as consultation and comparison, are commonplace in well-managed schools. Schools have been familiar with the value-for-money judgements made by inspectors for years. Best value reflects an attitude to management. You should explore the principles with the school as part of your evaluation of standards, the curriculum, and partnership with parents and management. Best value can be seen as a theme that runs across the different strands of inspection or school evaluation.

Bear in mind that working to these principles is an *expectation* of schools, not a *requirement* – as it is with local authorities. All inspection reports should indicate, however, the extent to which the work of the school reflects best value principles, summarising areas of strength and weakness. Whatever references are made in other areas of the report, your evaluation should be summarised in the leadership and management section.

If, on the evidence of the inspection, the performance of the school is not high enough, you are required to highlight your concerns in the report. These may include the extent to which the school does or does not apply best value principles effectively. These concerns must be set out in the section WHAT SHOULD THE SCHOOL DO TO IMPROVE FURTHER? and in the summary report. These concerns will be reflected in the inspection team's judgement about the school's capacity for improvement and its overall effectiveness, especially the summative judgement about whether the school is underachieving; has serious weaknesses in one or more areas; or is failing, or likely to fail, to give its pupils an acceptable standard of education and requires special measures.

BEST VALUE AND AUDIT

A feature of good school management is the use made of performance review to evaluate how well it is doing and to identify what action is needed to secure improvement. A key task of inspection is to evaluate the school's financial planning, and how it links its strategic use of resources, including specific grants and additional funding, with educational priorities. Many of these areas are covered in financial audit and you will need to make full use of the audit reports in coming to judgements about *costs* and *effectiveness* within the best value framework.

Audit and inspection are complementary processes. The following table identifies key common areas, based on the guidance on schemes of delegation under Fair Funding arrangements.[7] You will need to consider them in the light of evidence from inspection (including budget statements), taking full account of the school's most recent audit. The suggested format will help you organise the evidence and focus your judgements.

---

[7] See guidance issued by the Secretary of State under schedule 14 of the School Standards and Framework Act 1998.

Questions for audit	Areas for audit/inspection[8]	Questions for inspection
The focus of auditors will be on whether the governing body and the school:		*Inspectors will need to evaluate whether the governing body and school:*
• have set out clear delegation arrangements	**Delegation of powers to the headteacher**	• use delegation wisely
• maintain up-to-date inventories	**Control of assets**	• keep track of its resources
• have a register which is regularly updated and available for scrutiny	**Register of business interests**	• have a register available and whether its contents reveal any significant issues that require following up by others
• have a scheme to cover these arrangements which is used effectively within the best value framework	**Purchasing, tendering and contracting requirements**	• use these arrangements effectively and within the best value framework
• use buy-back services which fall within the scheme of delegation	**Buy-back of services from the LEA or elsewhere**	• effectively use support and other services purchased from the LEA or elsewhere
• regularly and properly have audits carried out	**Audits**	• have acted upon the recommendations to good effect
• submit the budget plan on time and accurately	**Budget plans**	• reflect in the budget plan the priorities set out in the school development plan; if not, why not?
• engage in any irregular spending and/or spending outside the scheme of delegation	**Spending for the purposes of the school**	• spend to reflect the school's purposes and identified priorities for improvement
• have arrangements for ensuring earmarked funds are used for their designated purposes	**Central funds and earmarking funds for designated purposes**	• monitor and evaluate their spending decisions within a best value framework
		• use earmarked funds only for their designated purposes
• undertake capital spending within regulations	**Capital spending**	• use capital spending appropriately and in line with priorities in the school development plan
		• monitor and evaluate capital spending decisions within a best value framework

---

[8] See guidance issued by the Secretary of State under schedule 14 of the School Standards and Framework Act 1998.

Questions for audit	Areas for audit/inspection	Questions for inspection
The focus of auditors will be on whether the governing body and the school:		*Inspectors will need to evaluate whether the governing body and school:*
• use their borrowing powers within the scheme of delegation	**Borrowing by schools**	• use borrowing wisely and in line with priorities set out in the school development plan
• ensure any income accrues to the budget • ensure that any cross-subsidy, for example from community or other use of facilities, has no net cost to the school's budget	**Income**	• ensure that arrangements for letting the building for community use benefit the school educationally and are in line with priorities set out in the school development plan
• have a plan for the use of budget surpluses	**Budget surpluses**	• plan to use budget surpluses wisely and in line with priorities set out in the school development plan
• have a justifiable deficit budget, that is licensed by the LEA and linked to an agreed plan for retrieving the budget deficit	**Budget deficits**	• have a deficit budget due to inefficient spending or for other reasons • have a plan for retrieving the deficit which is educationally justifiable and in line with priorities set out in the school development plan
• have a statement setting out what steps are to be taken to ensure best value, and whether the school's management and use of resources adhere to the declared intentions	**Best value**	• apply best value principles effectively in their management and use of resources

Evaluation of best value and financial management should be informed by the items in the right-hand column, although it may not be possible to investigate all of them rigorously.

USE OF PERFORMANCE INDICATORS

You will need to make full use of a range of performance indicators to judge whether the school is applying the best value framework consistently and effectively in its financial planning and management of resources. These indicators will be helpful if set alongside the school's own analysis of its performance (including any value-added analysis undertaken) and the school's account of the management decisions taken by governors, the headteacher and staff about the use of resources.

ANNEX 2

SCHOOLS REQUIRING SPECIAL MEASURES, SCHOOLS WITH SERIOUS WEAKNESSES, AND UNDERACHIEVING SCHOOLS

On every inspection, as a team, you must consider whether the school is failing, or likely to fail, to give its pupils an acceptable standard of education, and therefore requires special measures.

If you judge that the school is providing an acceptable standard of education, the next step is to consider whether it nevertheless has serious weaknesses.

You also need to consider whether the school, though not identified as having serious weaknesses, is judged to be underachieving.

These judgements must be reported using the prescribed wording, and specific procedures must be followed.

BACKGROUND

The School Inspections Act 1996 (the 1996 Act) states that: 'Special measures are required to be taken in relation to a school if the school is failing or likely to fail to give its pupils an acceptable standard of education'(section 13(9)).

Towards the end of an inspection, as a team, you must consider whether the school is failing, or likely to fail, to give its pupils an acceptable standard of education (Framework, paragraph 33). If you reach this view, and HMCI agrees, then special measures will be required.

If you reach the view that the school is providing its pupils with an acceptable standard of education, you should then and only then consider whether it nevertheless has serious weaknesses.

JUDGING THAT A SCHOOL REQUIRES SPECIAL MEASURES

The possibility that a school may be failing or likely to fail to give its pupils an acceptable standard of education should be considered initially during the pre-inspection analysis of data, indicators and other evidence about the school's performance.

It is uncomfortable coming to a judgement that a school is failing or likely to fail, but it is one which you must not shirk. You must not take the easier course represented by the judgement that the school has serious weaknesses if the evidence points to the conclusion that the school is not providing an acceptable standard of education.

Factors to consider

One feature alone is unlikely to result in a judgement that a school requires special measures, but where you find low standards and poor learning, risk to pupils or the likelihood of a breakdown of discipline, the school will normally require special measures.

The following questions are a guide to the judgement that a school requires special measures.

a. Education standards achieved:

i.	Is there low achievement in the subjects of the curriculum by the majority of pupils or consistently among particular groups of pupils?	Yes/No
ii.	Is there poor learning and progress in the subjects of the curriculum by the majority of pupils or consistently among particular groups of pupils?	Yes/No
iii.	Are there poor examination results?	Yes/No
iv.	Are the National Curriculum assessment and other accredited results poor?	Yes/No
v.	Is there regular disruptive behaviour?	Yes/No
vi.	Is there a breakdown of discipline?	Yes/No
vii.	Are there high levels of exclusions?	Yes/No
viii.	Are there significant levels of racial tension or harassment?	Yes/No
ix.	Is there poor attendance by a substantial proportion of pupils?	Yes/No
x.	Is there poor attendance by particular groups of pupils?	Yes/No
xi.	Is there a high level of truancy?	Yes/No

b. Quality of education provided:

i.	Is there a high proportion of unsatisfactory teaching?	Yes/No
ii.	Are there low expectations of pupils?	Yes/No
iii.	Is there failure to implement the National Curriculum?	Yes/No
iv.	Is there poor provision for pupils' spiritual, moral, social and cultural development?	Yes/No
v.	Are pupils at physical or emotional risk from other pupils or adults in the school?	Yes/No
vi.	Are there abrasive and confrontational relationships between staff and pupils?	Yes/No

c. The leadership and management of the school:

i.	Is the headteacher and/or the senior management team and/or the governors ineffective?	Yes/No
ii.	Is there significant loss of confidence in the headteacher by the staff and/or the parents and/or the governors?	Yes/No
iii.	Is there demoralisation and disenchantment amongst staff?	Yes/No
iv.	Are there high levels of staff turnover or absence?	Yes/No
v.	Is there poor management?	Yes/No
vi.	Is inefficient use made of the resources available to the school, including finance?	Yes/No
vii.	Does the school apply principles of best value in its use of resources?	Yes/No

You may also find the following forms useful in arriving at decisions:

EDUCATIONAL STANDARDS ACHIEVED	serious concern	some concern	no concern
Achievement in:			
English communication – including literacy			
Mathematics – including numeracy			
Science			
Design and technology			
Information technology			
History			
Geography			
Modern foreign languages			
Music			
Art			
PE			
In NC subjects or curriculum overall			
Religious education			
Other curricular provision			
National test/examination results			
Behaviour			
Level of exclusions			
Level of racial tension or harassment			
Attendance			
Truancy			

QUALITY OF EDUCATION PROVIDED	serious concern	some concern	no concern
Teaching			
Expectations of pupils			
Implementation of the National Curriculum			
Provision for pupils' SMSC development			
Pupils at physical/emotional risk from other pupils			
Pupils at physical/emotional risk from adults			
Relationships between staff and pupils			
LEADERSHIP AND MANAGEMENT OF THE SCHOOL			
Effectiveness of headteacher			
Effectiveness of other senior managers			
Effectiveness of the governors			
Confidence in the headteacher by staff			
Confidence in the headteacher by parents			
Confidence in the headteacher by governors			
Demoralisation and disenchantment among staff			
Level of staff turnover/absence			
Management/use made of available resources			
Principles of best value applied by the school			
School improvement since last inspection			
Ability to secure necessary improvements			

A school will be likely to fail if it:

- is close to the point where it would be judged to be failing;

- is declining rapidly in one or a number of important areas;

- is in decline and this is not being checked by the senior managers and appropriate authority;

- is in a precarious state where the management is ineffective and therefore the quality of education is likely to decline;

- has many weaknesses and had made insufficient progress since the last inspection.

Procedures to be followed

If the accumulating evidence suggests that the school may require special measures, you can get further guidance during office hours from the School Improvement Division in OFSTED (telephone 020 7421 6594). If, as a team, you reach the judgement that the school is failing or likely to fail, and therefore requires special measures, the registered inspector must:

- inform the School Improvement Division in OFSTED before the school is told of the judgement;

- before leaving the school at the end of the inspection, tell the headteacher orally either that in the view of the inspection team there are serious deficiencies and that the team is considering whether the school is failing, or likely to fail, to give its pupils an acceptable standard of education, or that the inspection team has reached a corporate judgement that the school is failing or likely to fail to give its pupils an acceptable standard of education;

- when giving oral reports to the senior management team and the appropriate authority, state that the corporate judgement of the inspection team is that the school is failing, or likely to fail, to give its pupils an acceptable standard of education. The following form of words could be used:

  I am of the opinion that special measures are required in relation to this school because it is failing (or likely to fail) to give its pupils an acceptable standard of education. In accordance with section 13(2) of the School Inspections Act 1996 I shall send a draft report to HMCI and will await his judgement on whether he agrees or not that the school requires special measures.

- explain that submission of the draft report to OFSTED may delay the issue of the report to the appropriate authority. The maximum delay is three months from the date when the report was due;

- use *Form 1* at the end of this section to inform the School Improvement Division in OFSTED of the team's decision;

- submit to OFSTED, but not to the school, the draft report and any other papers that are required as quickly as possible and by the agreed date, and always within five weeks of the end of the inspection.

What happens next?

HMI will consider the evidence and may visit the school before recommending to HMCI whether or not to agree that the school requires special measures. Whenever possible, if a visit is to take place, it will be within three working weeks of the inspection. The purpose of the visit will be to confirm or otherwise that special measures are required; HMI will not be re-inspecting the school.

If you are the registered inspector, you must ensure that all the evidence collected during the inspection is available for scrutiny by HMCI. It is probable that, on behalf of HMCI, the School Improvement Division will ask you to provide:

■ the school prospectus;

■ a plan of the school and a map showing its location;

■ timetables and a copy of any key that is necessary to be able to interpret the timetables;

■ the draft report and summary;

■ the completed *Record of Corporate Judgements* (including JRF grades), all completed *Inspection Notebooks* (including subject JRF grades), and *Evidence Forms*;

■ *Forms S1–S4*;

■ a note of the main issues raised at the parents' meeting and in the parents' questionnaire responses.

When HMI have scrutinised the evidence and, in some cases, visited the school, they report to HMCI. He will decide whether or not he agrees with the team's opinion and will tell you of his decision.

If HMCI agrees with the judgement that the school is failing or likely to fail, the following form of words should be used in the summary report:

> *In accordance with section 13(7) of the School Inspections Act 1996 I am of the opinion, and HMCI agrees, that special measures are required in relation to this school.*

If HMCI does not agree, the reasons will be explained and you will be given the opportunity to discuss HMCI's decision. Three options are open to you:

■ accept HMCI's decision and amend the report by removing the opinion that the school requires special measures, and then issue the report;

■ decide to issue the report without amendment. Special measures will not apply and you must then use the following form of words in the main findings of the report and in the summary:

> *In accordance with section 13(7) of the School Inspection Act 1996, I am of the opinion, but HMCI disagrees, that special measures are required in relation to this school.*

■ prepare further drafts for HMCI to consider, incorporating the opinion that the school is failing, or likely to fail. If HMCI still disagrees after considering subsequent drafts, you may decide to issue the report and summary without further amendment, but must state that HMCI disagrees with you using the form of words above. The report and summary must be substantially the same as the latest drafts sent to HMCI. Special measures will not apply.

JUDGING THAT A SCHOOL HAS SERIOUS WEAKNESSES

Factors to consider

If, as a team, you reach the view that the school is giving an acceptable standard of education, you should then consider whether or not it nevertheless has serious weaknesses in one or more areas of its work. In doing so, you should refer to the same characteristics as those you considered when deciding whether or not the school is giving an acceptable standard of education. You should make your judgements in the light of the findings as a whole, but should normally view the following weaknesses as significant:

- low standards of achievement and/or unsatisfactory learning and progress made, particularly in the core subjects;

- unsatisfactory teaching in about one in eight lessons;

- ineffective leadership and/or management.

Procedures to be followed

The registered inspector should tell the headteacher at the end of the inspection either that the team's view is that there are deficiencies and that it is considering whether the school has serious weaknesses, or that it has reached the judgement that the school has serious weaknesses. You must tell the School Improvement Division in OFSTED of your decision by telephone (020 7421 6594) before you tell the school, and subsequently send OFSTED the attached *Form 2*.

You should use a very clear form of words in the summary report. The words 'This school has serious weaknesses' must be included.

A copy of the final report should be sent to the School Improvement Division at the same time as it is sent to the school.

For further information and guidance about special measures or serious weaknesses, contact:

School Improvement Division
OFSTED
Alexandra House
33 Kingsway
London WC2B 6SE

Telephone: 020 7421 6594

JUDGING THAT A SCHOOL IS UNDERACHIEVING:

A judgement about whether a school is underachieving will be made, in appropriate circumstances, as part of both SHORT and FULL INSPECTIONS.

Factors to consider

The judgement should be made by considering:

- the effectiveness of the school;

- improvement since the last inspection;

- the performance of the school in comparison with schools in similar contexts.

It should be made on the basis of **performance data** and **inspection judgements** taken together.

Performance data

The performance data should include the following as applied to the highest Key Stage in the school:

- the school's results, compared with all schools nationally;

- the school's results, compared with schools in similar contexts, using QCA benchmarks;

- whether the school's average NC levels are improving over time, compared to the trend in national average NC levels.

For the majority of schools, the like-school comparison will be based on QCA free school meal bandings, as before.

You should consider the grade codes for national comparison and like-school comparisons, given in the *PICSI report*:

A* – very high in comparison with national average/average for similar schools

A – well above the national average/average for similar schools

B – above the national average/average for similar schools

C – average (in line with) the national average/average for similar schools

D – below the national average/average for similar schools

E – well below the national average/average for similar schools

E* – very low in comparison with the national average/average for similar schools

The performance data could, therefore, indicate elements of underachievement. Possible underachievement would be identified as part of the *Pre-Inspection Commentary* and provide a focus for the inspection. For example, for cases such as:

Grade for national comparison	Grade for comparison with schools in similar contexts	Trends in results
A*, A, B	D	Slower than national trends *or* no significant change over time
C	D/E	Slower than national trend
		No significant change over time

Inspection judgements

Evidence for underachievement found during the inspection will focus largely on aspects of teaching, learning, leadership and management, in conjunction with the hypotheses suggested by the data, as above. Significant pointers might be:

Teaching and learning

■ where the percentage of good or better teaching is low;

■ where the capacity of the teaching to challenge and inspire pupils is judged unsatisfactory, especially for higher-attaining pupils and other specific groups of pupils such as pupils with special educational needs or for whom English is an additional language, even if the teaching overall is satisfactory;

■ where the methods used to enable all pupils to learn effectively are judged unsatisfactory, although the teaching is judged satisfactory overall;

■ where the pupils' application of intellectual, physical or creative effort is judged unsatisfactory, although pupils' learning is judged satisfactory overall;

■ where the extent to which pupils show interest in their work, concentrate and think and learn for themselves is judged unsatisfactory, although pupils' learning is judged satisfactory overall.

Leadership and management

- where the monitoring, evaluation and development of teaching is judged unsatisfactory;

- where the shared commitment to improvement and the capacity to succeed are judged unsatisfactory;

- where the school's targets are not appropriate and/or progress towards meeting them is unsatisfactory.

School improvement

- where the judgement that the school has improved since the last inspection is barely satisfactory, overall, with specific and identifiable reservations based on the previous report and other sources of evidence.

The overall judgement that a school is underachieving would be based on:

- the performance data, which show the school's results are not as good as they could be;

- evidence that results are not improving sufficiently but not to the extent of being a serious weakness;

- significant concerns about aspects of **teaching, learning, leadership and management**, although these concerns are not acute enough to merit a judgement of serious weaknesses overall.

Procedures to be followed

The registered inspector should tell the headteacher at the end of the inspection either that the team's view is that it is considering whether the school is underachieving, or that it has reached the judgement that the school is underachieving. You must tell the School Improvement Division in OFSTED of your decision by telephone (020 7421 6594) before you tell the school, and subsequently send OFSTED the attached *Form 2*. You should use the words 'This school is underachieving' in the summary report. A copy of the final report should be sent to the School Improvement Division at the same time as it is sent to the school.

For further information and guidance about underachieving schools, contact:

School Improvement Division
OFSTED
Alexandra House
33 Kingsway
London WC2B 6SE

Telephone: 020 7421 6594

RECOMMENDATION FOR SPECIAL MEASURES

This form must be used by **all** lead inspectors to confirm the judgement that the school requires special measures. **Immediately the school has been informed of the decision, this form must be sent to:**

Head of the School Improvement Division
OFSTED
Alexandra House
Room 802
33 Kingsway
London WC2B 6SE

Inspection Number   ....

Date of inspection   ..../......./.......

School name   ....

Village/town   ....

Status   ....

Local Education Authority   ....

Name of lead inspector   ....

    [RgI] [AI] [HMI] (delete as appropriate)

Date when report and summary are due ..../......./.......

I am of the opinion that special measures are required in relation to this school, since it is failing/likely to fail to give its pupils an acceptable standard of education. The reasons for this opinion are:

1

2

3

4

(Please continue on separate sheet if necessary.)

I will send you drafts of the report and the summary by ..../......./.......

I confirm that I will report in these terms to the senior management team of the school and to the governors.

Signed   ....

Name (please print)   .... Date ..../......./........

Telephone number   ....

Address   ....

FORM 2

CONFIRMATION OF SERIOUS WEAKNESS OR THAT THE SCHOOL IS UNDERACHIEVING

This form must be used by **all** lead inspectors to confirm the judgement that the school has serious weaknesses **or** is underachieving. **Immediately the school has been informed of the decision, this form must be sent to:**

Head of the School Improvement Division
OFSTED
Alexandra House
Room 802
33 Kingsway
London WC2B 6SE

Date of inspection	......./......./.......
Date when report and summary are due	......./......./.......
I will send you the final report and the summary by	......./......./.......
School name	....
Village/town	....
Status	....
Local Education Authority	....
Name of lead inspector	....

[RgI] [AI] [HMI] (delete as appropriate)

Delete as appropriate:

I am of the opinion that this school is giving its pupils an acceptable standard of education, but it is a school with serious weaknesses. The reasons for this opinion are:

or

I am of the opinion that this school is underachieving. The reasons for this opinion are:

1

2

3

4

(Please continue on separate sheet if necessary.)

I confirm that I will report in these terms to the senior management team of the school and to the governors.

Signed ....

Name (please print) .... Date ..../........./........

Telephone number ....

Address ....

ANNEX 3

COMPLETING THE RECORD OF INSPECTION EVIDENCE

(A) COMPLETING THE *PRE-INSPECTION COMMENTARY*

What to include

The essential features of the *Pre-Inspection Commentary* are:

■ your preliminary views of the school in all areas of the *Evaluation Schedule*;

■ initial hypotheses, to be tested during the inspection, in each of these areas.

Using the *Pre-Inspection Commentary*

The evidence on which you base your views and hypotheses will come mainly from three sources, and you might find it helpful to structure your *Pre-Inspection Commentary* using these three areas. They are:

■ factual information from the *PICSI report* and other sources, such as *Forms S1* and *S2*;

■ the school's previous inspection report;

■ qualitative information you gain from *Forms S3* and *S4* and your visit to the school.

You should complete the *Pre-Inspection Commentary* in two stages. You will be able to begin writing the commentary when you have received the *PICSI report* and the completed inspection forms. The data contained in the *PICSI report* and *Forms S1* and *S2* will enable you to analyse the school's achievements in national tests. The headteacher's responses on *Forms S3* and *S4* will give you a picture of the school's own view of itself. You will then have sufficient knowledge of the school to put together a set of questions to ask the headteacher on the preliminary visit.

The information you obtain from the preliminary visit will enable you to complete the *Pre-Inspection Commentary* so that all team members have a clear picture of the school, in all areas of the *Evaluation Schedule*, before the inspection begins.

At the end of each section of the commentary you should include one or two key hypotheses for the inspection team to test out. Try to avoid long lists of hypotheses and focus on the 'big issues'. There is no need to include the reporting requirements or the criteria from the *Evaluation Schedule* because you will use these as a matter of course to evaluate the evidence in all inspections. What is needed is a small number of issues, which are drawn clearly from the evidence so far available and which relate specifically to the school being inspected.

In most cases these hypotheses will need to be followed up by all inspectors, and in a SHORT INSPECTION this will certainly be the case. In a FULL INSPECTION, individual team members may need to focus on particular issues and report back to the team at a suitable team meeting. You may find it helpful to indicate in the *Pre-Inspection Commentary* how an issue will be followed up, and by whom.

Style of writing

The *Pre-Inspection Commentary* needs to be concise and to the point. You will most likely write in continuous prose in short paragraphs. You should not rehearse all the evidence you have considered, which is contained in the *PICSI report*, inspection forms and the school's documentation. Your commentary should contain your views, so far, of what you have seen and discussed. The hypotheses should also be brief and to the point.

Extract from **Pre-inspection Commentary** *partially completed before the preliminary visit to the school*

Example before the school visit

2 How high are standards?   Interpretation of the school's results

Pre-inspection analysis of attainment:

Evaluation drawing on performance data, indicating Key Stages or groups of pupils, where relevant

Previous report:

- *Attainment on entry is average; attainment for U5s good in all areas of learning*

- *Standards in EN well above average in both Key Stages; in MA and SC above average in both*

- *In all other subjects EXCEPT IT attainment average (in line with national expectations)*

- *Literacy and numeracy skills used effectively across the curriculum*

- *IT skills NOT used effectively in other subjects*

- *Previous key issue to improve standards in IT and increase its use in other subjects*

PICSI report:

- *KS1 results for last year only average in reading and MA, above average in writing*

- *Similar schools comparisons show reading as below average, with writing and MA average*

- *Very low percentage of pupils attaining Level 3 in reading, writing and MA, and large number of Level W in reading*

- *Trends show drop in performance over last three years in reading and writing, with steady results in MA, despite decrease in FSM figure from 20 to 11 per cent*

(continued overleaf)

(Example continued)

- *KS2 results show better picture with EN, MA and SC results all well above average when compared with all schools and with similar schools*

- *Over one-third of pupils achieved Level 5 in EN, MA and SC*

- *MA and SC results show steady increase over three years, EN stay steady*

- *No differences between boys' and girls' results either in KS1 or KS2*

(IT and drop in results in KS1 to be followed up in detail in preliminary visit.)

Extract from the same Pre-Inspection Commentary, *showing the section written after the preliminary visit, and including the main issues for exploration during the inspection*

Example after the school visit

2 How high are standards? Interpretation of the school's results

Pre-inspection analysis of attainment:

Evaluation drawing on performance data, indicating Key Stages or groups of pupils, where relevant

Pre-inspection visit:

School's analysis of performance data good in its analysis by ethnic group, gender and teacher. No indication of value-added data yet, and little exploration of declining performance at end of KS1. HT indicates more pupils than usual with SEN in last year's Y2, now in Y3, but no convincing arguments that indicate school has got to grips with the issue. No monitoring of teaching to look at impact of teaching on learning in KS1, for example. No evaluation of effectiveness of demands made on high-attaining pupils or whether pupils with SEN are well supported.

School concerned that standards in IT still low. ICT network will have been up and running only six weeks before inspection. ICT strategy set up by HT; ICT co-ordinator is very good and staff fully involved at all stages. Its newness means that the impact on standards may be minimal yet.

Initial hypotheses and areas for further exploration:

The explanation of increased numbers of pupils with SEN in Y2 is likely to be only part of the picture of reduced performance at the end of KS1, particularly as there has also been a steady reduction in FSM rate. ALL team inspectors need to explore in detail what impact teaching has on learning and on standards in every KS1 observation, and pay particular attention to both ends of ability range.

Likely that standards in IT are still low, despite the work put in by staff and the new network. ALL team inspectors need to record use of ICT in every observation to give a picture of how well staff understand and have implemented the new policy. Team inspector covering IT needs to see whether improvement in standards are sufficient since last inspection, and whether current input is sufficiently demanding to raise them (or raise them further).

(B) COMPLETING THE *EVIDENCE FORM*

What to include

The *Evidence Form* is structured so that the same form can be used to record inspection evidence in four areas:

- **lesson observations** (coded **L**), including the observation of small groups or individual tuition;

- **analysis of pupils' work** (coded **A**), which might be undertaken independently of the pupils, or with the pupils present, to gain further insights into standards;

- **discussions** (coded **D**) with pupils, staff, governors and others;

- **any other evidence** (coded **O**), including observations of assemblies, registration periods, breaktimes, lunchtimes, arrival and departure from school and extra-curricular activities, and commentary on the school's documentation.

In writing each *Evidence Form*, you will need to complete the following parts:

- the **context** in which the form has been completed;

- the **evidence** you wish to record;

- when used for lesson observations, and optionally in other cases, **grades** for: teaching; learning; attainment; and attitudes and values;

- the **coding** boxes at the top.

Using the *Evidence Form*

Evidence Forms (EFs) are the key records of first-hand inspection evidence and your judgements on the basis of that evidence. You will need to refer to them when you identify strengths and weaknesses in your *Inspection Notebook*. They are also the source of illustrations for the inspection report.

When OFSTED's Inspection Quality Division monitors an inspection, the monitoring HMI may wish to look at the quality of evidence, judgement and grades recorded on *Evidence Forms*.

The context box

In the **context box**, put enough to describe the situation being recorded. If you are using the *EF* to record a discussion, say whom it is with and what it is about. If the *EF* is for a lesson or other observation, briefly describe what the teacher and pupils are doing, so that someone else could visualise the situation you observed. If you are recording your analysis of pupils' work, include sufficient detail to identify the work with the relevant subject or subjects and year or Key Stage.

Example of a context box for a lesson observation

Context:

Five different MA activities, with children grouped by ability. Objectives: introduce symmetry (with CLA); introduce multiplication (T); reinforce addition and subtraction (sheet and blocks); reinforce money problems (sheet); reinforce number bonds (textbook). T and CLA support all groups following initial focused input.

The evidence box

In the **evidence box** you should record the evidence you have collected and your judgements on the basis of that evidence. Each *EF* should contain:

- sufficient **evidence** to support the judgement(s) you make, in that anyone reading the evidence would be very likely to come to the same judgement;

Example of a lesson observation – recording evidence

Evidence:

Able to recall the terms tributary, source and meander and explain what they mean. Demonstrate a clear understanding of the concept of tributary and apply their knowledge by gathering data from a published map to identify tributaries of the River Severn. Attainment in line with pupils of this age.

Y4 geography observation   **Attainment – Grade 4**

- a strong **focus on strengths and weaknesses,** and what makes them strengths and weaknesses, with less emphasis on that which is satisfactory but has no major positive or negative features;

Example of a lesson observation – recording strengths and weaknesses

Evidence:

Lively relationship and good way of asking children questions about stories to do with journeys. Children respond with wide range of stories they know. Good questioning technique challenges children's understanding, involves individuals checking their own comprehension and keeps them well focused (S). Tendency to focus children's listening on teacher's interpretation of what children have said, rather than on listening to each other (W).

YR English observation   **Teaching and learning – Grade 3**

■ **illustrations** which can be drawn on by you or other inspector when writing text for the report, particularly of strengths and weaknesses;

Example of a lesson observation – recording illustrations

Evidence:

Pupils highly motivated when working against the clock as they consolidate their mental arithmetic. Sensible when checking one another, and when using stop-watches. Good concentration throughout, self-set targets for improvement and excitement when targets met.

Y4 mathematics lesson   **Attitudes and behaviour – Grade 2**

■ **judgements** made on the basis of the evidence and, in the case of lesson observations, summary judgements on teaching and learning, attainment, attitudes and behaviour;

Example of a lesson observation – recording judgements

Evidence:

Objectives of lesson simple and clear. The music was carefully chosen to emphasise fast playing of instruments. Hand-clapping task ensured that every pupil was able to participate very quickly. Clapping outcomes showed that pupils had no difficulty with this task but the further challenges needed to move their learning on were not there.

Y1 music lesson   **Teaching – Grade 4**

■ **explanations** that justify why things are as they are.

Example of a lesson observation – recording explanations

Evidence:

Pupils gained much from this session because they knew what they were expected to learn, had a good knowledge of the story's format and gave well thought-out suggestions for missing words which were taken on and developed in discussion with other pupils.

Y4/5/6 literacy class   **Learning – Grade 3**

You may wish additionally to use part of this space to record, for example, the way pupils with special educational needs learn, or how pupils with English as an additional language are supported by the use of information and communications technology (ICT) in all subjects. This focused approach is most effective when used consistently by all members of the inspection team in every lesson observation.

The grade boxes

When you enter **grades** at the foot of the form, make sure they match the judgements in the text above about teaching and learning, attainment, and pupils' attitudes and behaviour. You should always grade lesson observations. You may find it helpful to grade *EF*s that record your analysis of pupils' work, and any *EF*s coded 0 in which there is an element of teaching, such as in an assembly or in some extra-curricular activities.

In **lesson observations** you must always grade **teaching, learning,** and pupils' **attitudes and behaviour.** In most cases you will use Grades 1–7 but you may need to use 0 if there is too little evidence to make a secure judgement. On very rare occasions, you may need to use 8 to indicate that it is not appropriate to enter a grade. Wherever possible, you should enter a grade for attainment. If you feel you do not have the expertise to make a judgement about attainment, for example if you are a lay inspector, it is acceptable to leave the attainment grade blank.

You should try to use the full range of grades. So, for example, if pupils' learning in a lesson is exemplary and you cannot see how it could be improved, award a Grade 1 and make sure that the text on the *EF* supports this grade.

Filling in the coded boxes at the top of the form

Every time you write an *EF* you need to code, where possible, the sections at the top of the form. The diagram shows what is needed. Further details are provided on the CD-ROM accompanying this *Handbook*.

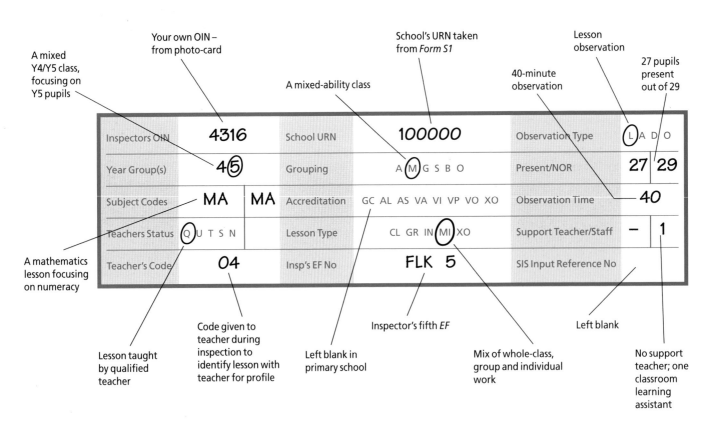

Style of writing

There is no prescribed format for completion of *EFs*. Effective writing could be in continuous prose or in note form; it could list strengths and weaknesses separately or cover the same ground within a single piece of text. What matters is that the *EF* communicates to others the essential features of what has been seen or discussed.

In **lesson observations,** the pieces of evidence you obtain for teaching and learning are often inextricably linked. When you write the *EF* you should integrate these two areas whenever you can. You may wish to note particular points in each area that help you reach the two separate grades needed. If the grades for teaching and learning are different, for example if the teacher did all he or she could but other factors meant that pupils' learning was not graded as highly, you need to explain why they are different.

Example of a lesson observation – recording differences in judgements

Evidence:

Teacher's planning good and objectives explained to pupils. Group supported by teacher worked well because teacher's open questioning gave good lead-in to designing the experiment to test solubility and highlighted safety aspects. Two groups, each supported by a classroom assistant who had not been briefed beforehand, made little progress until they developed their own ideas from observations of other pupils and eventually succeeded with the task.

Y5/6 science observation   **Teaching – Grade 5; Learning – Grade 4**

In the **analysis of pupils' work** you should primarily use the *EF* to give a clear picture of pupils' attainment. You can use the *EF* to record the attainment of different groups of pupils and your exploration of differences in the standards achieved by pupils of different gender or ethnic background. You should also try, where you can, to bring out any evidence about teaching, pupils' learning and their attitudes.

Example of recording the analysis of pupils' work

Context:

Extract from the analysis of KS2 work in English

Evidence:

The range of written work is impressive and includes poetry, extended narrative, short story, newspaper and letters. A very good progressive development of narrative style. Progress from Y3–Y6 is reflected in the sophistication of vocabulary used, the use of punctuation, the use of dialogue and the development of a strong individual style.

No differences noted between attainment or progress of pupils from different ethnic groups, but those with EAL do not have the breadth of vocabulary or security of sentence structure of their peers in Y3. Boys do not produce the range or quality of work done by girls in Y3 or Y4. Both these differences have been almost eliminated by end of Y6. The stimulus material reflects good teaching and some challenging materials (e.g., Romeo and Juliet).

(continued overleaf)

(Example continued)

The annotation sheet used by teachers to assess the work is excellent, with learning intentions, activity details, children's learning outcomes and next steps. Next steps filled in particularly well and targeted at improvement in specific areas (e.g., 'Your stories need more description and less speech where you want to move the story on faster').

Overall: level of work well above that expected for their age

When you write about **discussions** with pupils, staff, governors or others, you should record the key points of the discussion, not try to transcribe all of what was said. This is often easier if the discussion takes place using a set of headings designed specifically for that occasion. At the end of the discussions, if there is time, you might find it helpful to go briefly through what you have written to check you have the main points accurately recorded.

Example of a report of a discussion with ICT co-ordinator

Context:

Extract from a record of a discussion with the ICT co-ordinator about leadership and management role of co-ordinator

Evidence:

Headteacher and governors had listened and had recognised school's needs as presented to them. HT had helped plan the school's ICT strategy. Co-ord felt empowered by the way they had delegated responsibility.

Co-ord keeps governors informed, and feels secure in relationship with governing body. Many fruitful discussions with HT.

Involves staff in decision-making and used skills audit of all staff and governors to identify training needs. Didn't move on with issues until knew staff ready. Staff very responsive and responsible in tackling their own INSET needs.

Cost-effectiveness: investment in ICT has paid off in terms of raised expectations of teachers and dramatic increase in standards. Impact on standards has been across the curriculum, e.g., building bridges in DT in Y3, composing in MU in Y2, presentation of writing in all years and of data in MA in Y3–Y6

Judgement from evidence: co-ord has clear picture of strengths and weaknesses in ICT across the school; HT and governors have given co-ord clear brief to raise standards; co-ord has well-devised plan to bring about improvement; action taken is monitored and evaluated; approach is leading to improvements in standards and is cost-effective; overall, very good.

(C) COMPLETION OF *INSPECTION NOTEBOOKS*

What to include

On FULL INSPECTIONS and on SHORT INSPECTIONS, where it is used, the *Inspection Notebook* should always include:

- judgements in as many areas of the *Evaluation Schedule* as possible for which you have evidence, expressed as strengths and weaknesses;

- references to the *Evidence Forms* which form the basis for these judgements, and which can be used to illustrate them, if needed, in the inspection report;

- an overall evaluation under each *Evaluation Schedule* heading for which you have evidence.

When you are inspecting a subject or more than one subject during a FULL INSPECTION, your *Notebook* should additionally contain:

- a section on pre-inspection evidence about those subjects, written using the guidance given above for completing the *Pre-Inspection Commentary*;

- a summary of the feedback you intend to give to the co-ordinator for each subject you are inspecting, at or towards the end of the inspection;

- grades for the judgement recording statements in each of the subjects you are responsible for;

- the time you have spent on firsthand inspection in the school.

In a FULL INSPECTION, when you are responsible for writing aspects or subject sections of the report, the *Inspection Notebook* will also contain:

- the draft text of your contributions to the inspection report, usually completed after the final team meeting.

Using the *Inspection Notebook*

Each inspector, including the registered inspector, must complete an *Inspection Notebook* in a FULL INSPECTION, and the completed form will be entered into the inspection software. You may use one in a SHORT INSPECTION if you find it convenient to do so, but its contents will not be entered into the inspection software. It will, however, form part of the evidence base for the inspection.

The *Inspection Notebook* is for you to record your own views and judgements on the evidence you have collected. You should use it after you have reflected on the evidence from a number of sources. For example, after seeing several lessons on the first day of an inspection, you will probably feel you have sufficient evidence about teaching to record your views and make some tentative judgements about the quality of teaching. You should express your views as strengths and weaknesses. There is no need to include extensive commentary on things which are satisfactory. These views would form the basis of your contribution to the inspection team's discussions about teaching at a team meeting. You would be able to illustrate your points by referring back to the evidence on your *Evidence Forms*. For this reason, you will need to include a reference to the source(s) of evidence against each judgement recorded.

You will probably find that, in some areas of the *Evaluation Schedule*, you will be combining evidence from a range of different sources before writing in your *Inspection Notebook*. For example, your views on pupils' behaviour will come from *Evidence Forms* covering lessons, what you have seen outside lessons and discussions with staff and pupils.

In FULL INSPECTIONS, where you are inspecting more than one subject or aspect, you will need to structure your *Notebook* according to the subjects and/or aspects you are responsible for. If you are responsible for more than one subject, you will need to complete a judgement recording form for each. Your evidence should incorporate any observations or other evidence of 'your' subjects accrued by other members of the team. Their evaluations in your focus subjects should therefore be represented in your *Notebook*, together with the JRF for each of those subjects.

Whether you fill in your *Inspection Notebook* by hand or using a computer, you should treat it as a running commentary, which can be modified and added to as the inspection proceeds.

Towards the end of the inspection, you will need to make an overall evaluation of the evidence you have obtained under each heading in the *Evaluation Schedule*. You will also need to make sure that all the strengths and weaknesses recorded represent your final considered judgements, as these will be entered into the inspection software with the other inspection information.

You will also need to record the source(s) from which you derived each judgement. This will be a reference to one or more *Evidence Forms*, possibly from other inspectors on the team. In a FULL INSPECTION you will need copies of these forms if you are writing a subject or aspect, so that you can refer to them after the inspection has finished.

When an inspection is monitored by OFSTED's Inspection Quality Division, the monitoring HMI may wish to look at the quality of evaluations and judgements contained in *Inspection Notebooks*.

The subject judgement recording form

Towards or at the end of each FULL INSPECTION, you will need to enter grades in each subject inspected for the judgement recording statements at the back of the *Inspection Notebook*. The numbering follows that of the school judgement recording statements in the *Record of Corporate Judgements*. The grades should fall naturally into place from the judgements you have recorded in the earlier pages of the *Inspection Notebook*. If assigning a grade is difficult, it probably indicates that you have not already made or not recorded a clear judgement. In these circumstances you are advised to go back to consider the judgement itself, making use of the strengths and weaknesses you have recorded and, if necessary, referring to *Evidence Forms*.

Style of writing

You use the *Inspection Notebook* to record judgements, summarise your views and point to the evidence on which they are based. It should be written very concisely, therefore. It should consist of:

- single-sentence statements, or the equivalent in note form;

- coded references to *Evidence Forms*, using the code entered in the box at the top of each relevant form.

3 How well are pupils and students taught?   Teaching and learning

What is the quality of teaching and what is its impact?

Strengths and weaknesses from the inspection, indicating groups of pupils and Key Stages where relevant, and an overall evaluation

	Sources of evidence:

Foundation – strengths:

• Questioning well used to check children's understanding	All U5 EFs
• Well-planned lessons but flexible approach to match children's needs	All U5 EFs
• Very good management of pupils, moves lessons on at good pace without undue pressure on children	EFs JS6, JS8
• Very good interaction with children, encouraging less-confident to take part in active discussion	EFs JS6, JS8
• Very good development of sound recognition, aural and written. Higher-attainers introduced to more complex words and able to explain their meanings, e.g., myth, lynch	EFs JS12, JS8

Foundation – weaknesses:

• Use of extra adults in classroom unfocused	EFs JS8, JS12

KS1:

• No particular strengths or weaknesses in consistently satisfactory teaching

KS2 – strengths:

• Well-planned lessons, with objectives clear to pupils. Pupils always clear about the focus for the activity	EFs JS1, JS4
• Practical activities provide good opportunities to develop investigative skills	EFs JS1, JS4

Overall evaluation:

Very good teaching in U5s gives them many opportunities to develop skills, through very effective questioning and management of pupils. Sound teaching in KS1. Good teaching in KS2 linked to clarity of objectives.

(D) COMPLETION OF THE *RECORD OF CORPORATE JUDGEMENTS*

What to include

The *Record of Corporate Judgements* for your inspection must include:

- corporate judgements of the inspection team in each area of the *Evaluation Schedule*;

- agreed grades for each of the judgement recording statements required in your inspection;

- agreed grades for each of the additional judgement recording statements *P1–P10*;

- agreed grades and, where necessary, reasons for changes of grade, to the similar school comparisons;

- statements and, where necessary, reasons for your decisions about whether the school requires special measures, has serious weaknesses or is underachieving;

- a summary of the extent and range of the inspection evidence.

Using the *Record of Corporate Judgements*

A single *Record of Corporate Judgements (RCJ)* is used in each inspection. It is completed at team meetings towards the end of an inspection and/or at the final team meeting after the inspection. You should use the *Record of Corporate Judgements* to record the team's agreed judgements and point to the evidence on which they are based. When parts of the *RCJ* are completed at an earlier team meeting, the contents of these parts will need to be confirmed at the final team meeting after the inspection. Because, as the registered inspector, you will be managing these meetings, it will be helpful if the actual recording is carried out by another member of the team, leaving you free to focus on the team's judgements.

The order of the pages in the *Record of Corporate Judgements* is designed to support the final inspection team meeting by moving from the detail of what was known before the inspection, through the evidence base collected during the inspection, to the evaluation of the effectiveness of the school. In short, you are expected to use the *Record of Corporate Judgements* to bring all your judgements together and reach some overall conclusions.

The main strengths and weaknesses are expressed, in draft form, as they will appear in the relevant boxes in the summary of the inspection report, namely WHAT THE SCHOOL DOES WELL and WHAT COULD BE IMPROVED. The *Record of Corporate Judgements* also gives space to draft the matters that the 'appropriate authority' must include in its post-inspection action plan. These should match exactly the entries in the section WHAT COULD BE IMPROVED.

The final team meeting represents the culmination of the collection of evidence, testing out hypotheses and reaching tentative judgements, which are then confirmed, or otherwise. The *Record of Corporate Judgements* is a way of ensuring that the team's agreed judgements are recorded so that they can be used as the basis for writing the inspection report. Individual inspectors will be able to contribute a range of strengths or weaknesses in each section of the *Evaluation Schedule* and the team needs to weigh these up, making reference to the evidence base where necessary, to reach corporate judgements. Once these judgements have been agreed, it is a relatively easy task for the team to assign grades to the judgement recording statements.

You will also need to record the source from which the judgement stems. This might be a reference to an *Inspection Notebook* or it might be a reference to one or more *Evidence Forms*. If you refer to an *Inspection Notebook*, you will need to ensure that it contains the reference to the *Evidence Forms*.

You should use the *Record of Corporate Judgements* carefully and record only the significant points you wish to include in the inspection report. You should record all the required judgements you will need for the summary report, so that when you come to write it, all the necessary information will be to hand. When you, and in some cases others, come to write the commentary section of the report, you will need to expand these points, drawing on explanatory and illustrative material from *Inspection Notebooks* and *Evidence Forms*.

The school judgement recording form

You will need to end your discussions of each section of the *Evaluation Schedule* by grading the judgement recording statements relevant to your inspection. In SHORT INSPECTIONS, the statements will be those at the top of the list of statements, printed in bold typeface. In FULL INSPECTIONS, you will also need to grade the more detailed statements printed in italic typeface.

If assigning a grade is difficult, it probably indicates that a clear corporate judgement has not been reached and you are advised to go back to consider the judgement itself, making use of the strengths, weaknesses and illustrations contributed by members of the inspection team. Having reconsidered the judgement, and possibly having re-written it in the *Record of Corporate Judgements*, the grade should fall naturally into place.

The ten judgement recording statements in the *Record of Corporate Judgements* not connected directly with an *Evaluation Schedule* heading (*P1–P10*) are pointers to what the report contains, not judgements in themselves. For example, *Statement P1* is not about whether the attainment of boys and girls is different, but about whether the report contains such a judgement. You can, therefore, usually answer these straightforwardly with *Yes* or *No*.

You will also need to consider as a team whether the grades in the *PICSI report* which describe the school's performance in relation to similar schools will be included in the report as they are printed in the *PICSI report* or if they will be modified. If you feel there is substantial and compelling evidence to suggest that a grade different by one grade from that given in the *PICSI report* is more appropriate, then this should be entered and an explanation given. If you feel that, in an exceptional case, a change of two or more grades, or the omission of the grade, is necessary, you must additionally inform the Inspection Quality Division of OFSTED of this, giving the reasons for your decision, and submit the supporting evidence.

Guidance on reaching conclusions about whether the school requires special measures, has serious weaknesses, or is underachieving, is given in Annex 2.

The summary of the extent of inspection evidence at the end of the *Record of Corporate Judgements* is completed by collating the times and evidence bases from each *Inspection Notebook* used. In SHORT INSPECTIONS, you will need to ask the other members of the inspection team to inform you of their contribution as it will not always be recorded in an *Inspection Notebook*.

Style of writing

Because the *Record of Corporate Judgements* is a summary of the team's inspection judgements, it should be written very concisely. It should consist of:

■ single-sentence statements, or the equivalent in note form;

■ coded references to *Inspection Notebooks* and *Evidence Forms*, using the entries in the bottom centre box at the top of each relevant *Evidence Form*.

Example of a page from a Record of Corporate Judgements

7 How well is the school led and managed?

How effectively do the leadership and management of the school contribute to pupils' achievements?

Main strengths and weaknesses, indicating groups of pupils and Key Stages, where relevant, and sources of evidence, and an overall evaluation

	Sources of evidence:
Strengths:	
• *Very well led, with some aspects outstanding: exceptional vision and commitment to raising standards; setting clear agenda for senior staff in their development work*	*EFs JS10, PD6, PD12, JS2, PIC*
• *Very well managed, delegation very effective, keeps regular track of development work of senior managers*	*EFs JS10, PD7, JS2*
• *Governors fully involved, knowledgeable; trust head but challenge as appropriate*	*EFs PD9, JS10*
• *In-depth evaluations based on detailed and thorough analysis of data, and school well aware of its own strengths and weaknesses*	*EFs PD9, JS10, TP3*
• *School improvement plan has strengths in identification of professional development needs based on thorough evaluation of need and linking these to evaluation strategies*	*EFs PD9, JS2*
Weaknesses:	
• *Firsthand monitoring of teaching not targeted on identification of areas for improvement, and not specifically linked to evaluation of initiative*	*EF PD7*
• *School improvement plan weak on cost-effectiveness, and does not link evaluation of outcomes (i.e., improvement in standards) to costs*	*EFs PD9, JS2*

Overall evaluation:

Leadership of the school is very good, with the vision provided by the headteacher outstanding. It is well managed, with good delegation and evaluation. Some improvements are needed in development planning and the monitoring of teaching.

ANNEX 4

NATIONAL EDUCATIONAL INITIATIVES

Increasingly, inspections will take place in schools that are involved in a network, project or scheme which receives specific funding to promote particular educational goals such as raising standards.

The inspection report must refer to such involvement in the INFORMATION ABOUT THE SCHOOL section. You should also report on any impact on quality and standards in the school, which accrues from involvement in the project.

In some inspections, much more detailed evaluation of the project and its impact will feature through section 9 of the *Evaluation Schedule*. In such cases, additional time will be added to the inspection contract, and OFSTED will provide supplementary guidance on the inspection of the issue concerned.

This annex sets out background information about three initiatives in which some primary and nursery schools are involved.

1. EARLY EXCELLENCE CENTRES

Purpose

Early Excellence Centres (EECs) aim to be models for the development of integrated early years services. They aim to bring together high-quality early learning, childcare and family support services for those children and parents who need them. They should be catalysts for the development of good practice in the areas and regions they serve, and for spreading new ideas and providing innovative services.

Key features

Early Excellence Centres usually incorporate one or more nursery schools or classes. They will:

- be multidisciplinary, by drawing together education, care, adult education, private and voluntary providers and employers to collaborate in providing one-stop services;

- have a strong emphasis on staff training and development, and outreach support for parents and other providers;

- include support for parents who need help with parenting skills and literacy, for example enabling parents to attend classes in the same centre as their children;

- allow parents who work or are training for work to have access to integrated education and childcare for their children;

- ensure that parents of children with special educational needs can look forward to early assessment of their child's needs and a planned programme of linked provision, including support for the parents themselves, where appropriate.

Inspection focus

You should evaluate only the direct impact of the activities of the EEC on the educational aspects of the nursery or primary school you are inspecting, as set out in the *Evaluation Schedule*. Features may include the enhanced involvement of parents, students or others in the education provided. You must not evaluate the work or impact of other professional services, such as medical, social or psychological services, in relation to the school.

2. EDUCATION ACTION ZONES

Purpose

Education Action Zones (EAZs) are a key part of government policy to raise standards in areas which face challenging circumstances in terms of underachievement or disadvantage. They receive extra funding from government, business and industry. A partnership forum, which sets out an action plan to raise standards, runs them. They are free from some statutory requirements.

Key features

Education Action Zones:

- are established in less favoured parts of the country;

- invite an innovative contribution from business;

- have government funding of at least £250,000 per annum matched by business funding;

- address local problems;

- focus on teaching and learning;

- may suspend the National Curriculum;

- could change teachers' pay and conditions;

- may employ Advanced Skills Teachers;

- are organised in different ways.

Centrally, they exist to raise educational achievement in the areas they serve.

Inspection focus

Evaluate how particular EAZ initiatives contribute to the effectiveness of the leadership and management of the school. For example, there may be:

- mentors from business working with headteachers;

- business expertise to improve teachers' skills at middle-management level;

- business help in target-setting.

You must evaluate the contribution of an EAZ against your assessment of its prime purpose, the likelihood or actuality of the EAZ raising standards achieved.

3. EXCELLENCE IN CITIES

Purpose

Excellence in Cities provides a new framework for inner-city schools. The initiative aims to raise standards and aspirations in bigger cities. It is designed to ensure that every gifted pupil is stretched and that a full range of special needs is met. The aim of the programme is to extend diversity and excellence by tackling low expectations and any other barriers to learning.

Key features

The initiative includes:

- a radical approach to the needs of gifted and talented children;

- an encouragement to schools to use setting to meet individual aptitudes and abilities;

- developing new tests to stretch the most able;

- tackling disruption in schools through learning support units;

- providing the support of learning mentors to every pupil who needs one;

- establishing new university summer schools for 16–17-year-olds in the inner-city.

Inspection focus

Like EAZs, the purpose of the initiative is to raise standards. If you are inspecting a school which is part of the Excellence in Cities initiative, your evaluation should give a clear view of the initiative's effect on the standards achieved and on any other factors which have an impact on standards, such as teaching and leadership and management. You should be able to identify positive benefits from the initiative across all aspects of the school. In particular, this should be evident in the standards achieved by gifted and talented pupils.

INDEX

Printed in the United Kingdom for The Stationery Office   TJ C15 4/00

OFSTED – Inspecting Schools Series: effective from January 2000

0 11 3501099 – *Handbook for Inspecting Primary and Nursery Schools*
0 11 3501102 – *Handbook for Inspecting Secondary Schools*
0 11 3501110 – *Handbook for Inspecting Special Schools and Pupil Referral Units*

Users may find the following list of frequently asked questions and their answers helpful.

Q. How do I install the CD-ROM?
A. The only aspect of the CD-ROM that might need installing on your computer is the Adobe®
Acrobat® Reader. Instructions on how to install this are provided in the booklet in the plastic wallet. You
will need to be sure to uninstall old versions of the Reader first (*see next question*).

If you are a Mac user and need to install Reader, please contact tech.supp@theso.co.uk as there is a
problem with the Reader installation files provided for Macs. Alternatively, you can download a version
of the Reader from the Adobe website: www.adobe.com

Once you have installed the Reader, you view the files in much the same way as you would use Word,
for example to view documents.

Q. Why do I receive an error message about creating thumbnails?
A. The error message usually appears when you have an older version of the Reader installed on your
computer. Please note that the forms have been designed for viewing with version 3 of the Reader. If
you have version 2.1, you will need to upgrade. Always uninstall any older versions of the software
before installing newer ones. (If you have not done this you will still see the error message.) You can
uninstall by using the "Add/Remove Programs" facility in the control panel, or by using the "Uninstall
Acrobat Reader" function on the Programs/Adobe Acrobat Reader menu. When you have uninstalled
you can proceed with the installation of version 3 or 4 from the CD-ROM. Please see the instructions
on installing Acrobat provided in the booklet accompanying the CD-ROM.

Q. I can't complete the forms electronically. How do I do this?
A. Please note that the forms on the CD-ROM, which accompanies these books, are **not** intended to be
completed on screen. **The CD-ROM was designed to allow the forms to be printed off for
completion by hand.**

Q. When I copy the forms to Word I lose the formatting. How do I get round this?
A. You should not try to copy the forms data to any other application. However, for details of how to edit
the letters electronically, please see the following instruction.

Q. How can I customise the "Draft letter for the appropriate authority"?
A. To re-use the text of the letters on the CD-ROM, you will need to copy and paste the letter into your
word processing package using the following procedure:

1.   With the letter on screen, from the "Edit" menu choose "Select All", re-select the "Edit" menu and
     choose "Copy".
2.   Next, open a new document in your word processing package and paste the copied letter into this
     new document. The letter can now be edited by the user and saved on their PC.

Q. My printer won't print the forms off the CD-ROM. Why, and what can I do about it?
A. Portable Document Files can be quite resource-intensive when it comes to printing; some printers
simply cannot cope and will have an "overflow" problem. The only way to overcome this problem is to
try different printers.

Please note that users who continue to experience difficulty with printing and installation should contact
their own PC support or IT unit.

OFSTED
The Stationery Office
March 2000